Unify Your Marketing

5 Steps to Build Your Marketing
in the Right Order So Your Business Can Soar!

By BEAR WADE

Published by Unify Creative Agency
UnifyYourMarketing.com
Unify-Agency.com
BearWade.com

Bulk order for your team? Email: Hello@Unify-Agency.com.

ISBN: 9780578952352
ISBN EPUB: 9780578952376
Printed in the United States of America

Special Thanks To:

*Amy Dunn for all of your contributions to making
this book a reality and for the constant cheer-leading
I needed to make this book happen!*

*Jennifer Wade for supporting me in all my creative endeavors.
This year has been an amazing transformation for us!*

Cover design by: Bear Wade & Amy Dunn

Graphic layout by: Haley Montgomery

Edited by: Ashley Beck & Steffanie Moyers

Additional contributions by: Jamie Wentz

Website design by: Bear Wade & Mike McAllister

*Also, I appreciate the work we've done together:
Bethany Dreher, Paul Dreher, Kevin Gallagher,
Joe Lampe, Dennis Fry, Dave Zaegle, Jeff Berger,
Jason Pride, Meg Erke, Sherman Lee, Candice Wassell,
April Abbonizio, Robert Hummert, Keith Pittillo,
Michael Kerber, Erin Quirarte, Mo Bin Masoud, and Matt Olin.*

*A special thanks to my supportive family, Bob & Renée Wade,
Foster Wade, Davin Wade, Chelsea & Jason Guerin,
and Peg & Dale Jones.*

CONTENTS

UNIFY STEP 5

SCALING 236

ICON KEY

Throughout this book you'll notice that I've highlighted different elements that can be of extra benefit to you. Follow these icons throughout the book to enhance your ability to successfully achieve business success.

 EXERCISE

I have placed exercises throughout, where you can put your newly-learned knowledge to work for your business!

 KEY TAKEAWAY

At the end of each chapter we will summarize the main points. Come back to these while you work through each step.

 PRO TIP

There are more insights to be found in the margins!

 CONSIDER HIRING A CONTRACTOR

Wondering when it makes sense to hire out? Look for these icon at the start of chapters.

 CASE STUDY

I will dive deeper into a topic using a real-life example from my client work.

 DOWNLOAD

There are tons of resources, exercises, and gems of knowledge available for you to download at UnifyYourMarketing.com

LET'S GET A QUICK WIN

6 key pain points & solutions you can implement today.

Business owners, are you ready for a quick win?

It's time to identify your immediate pain point and an action plan to overcome it.

Pain points are a challenge that holds your business back from progressing. It's possible that you feel something dragging you down, but maybe you're having trouble putting your finger on it.

Or maybe you know exactly what it is and have tried and failed at a lot of solutions. I got ya. I get stuck too. It is extremely stressful, isn't it?

I believe that every business has a pain point that they have to overcome. No business is perfect and every business owner is working to address their pain points to keep the ship afloat.

In order to get to the next level, you have to both name your pain points and identify a plan to work through them.

Before we jump into all of the steps, let's get a 30,000-foot view of your business. This vantage point will help you identify any pain points that are critically impacting your business and need to be triaged now.

The six most common pain points:

- Failing Business Model
- Poor Leadership Communication
- Lack of Brand
- Lack of Promotion
- Lack of Sales Funnel
- Undefined Systems

Failing Business Model

A poor business model is when your business doesn't have:

1. A predictable way to bring in customers
2. The ability to fulfill its orders
3. A method to turn one-time customers into repeat customers.

Does this sound familiar? You are **constantly** looking for more customers, for example, a wedding photographer who is constantly hunting for more couples to work with.

How about a residential roofer who re-roofs a house and then has to wait for the next hail storm to be in demand again and book any work? It is another business model that relies heavily on customer acquisition.

Sure you can make TONS of money in these two industries, but you have to have a predictable advertising system to reach new customers time and time again.

You don't want to be in a one-off business that doesn't have recurring revenue. If you are coming up with ways to turn what you do into ongoing packages, or have sales cycles built into them, that will help your business sustainability.

Think about your local grocery store. The goal is to get you in there once a week, if not more, and get you to buy the same things over and over because that helps grow their profits on a repeatable basis. I'm sure you "just came in for milk," but guess what? The milk is located at the very back of the store so that you have to walk past all of the other delicious and practical options before you get there. That's not a coincidence, it's a strategy.

There are some business models that are easier to manage than others, and it all depends on your personality as a leader, your natural tendencies, and the team you have around you. Just because you have a current business model in place doesn't mean you can't change it. So consider how your business operates and adjust it to win.

My business model keeps evolving

When I was starting out in business, I started right out of college. Armed with a degree in photography, I focused on booking gigs to photograph weddings. It is in the general public psyche that when you have a wedding that you hire a photographer, so it seemed natural to me that people were looking for my service.

Photographing the wedding was great. Everyone's happy (usually) and dressed well, and there's cake. The grind came from having to find new clients for every gig, and you could never sell that client the same package again. There was no repeat business with that model. On top of that, the work was seasonal for the most part. Two strikes against it!

I spent so much time and energy working to find new couples to photograph. My marketing budget was a small start out, and it was hard to stand out in a market that was pretty saturated.

Eventually, I realized the business model wasn't working and I sought out new revenue streams.

What can you do to adjust your business model so that your company is structured to be sustainably profitable?

If this pain point resonates with you, consider reviewing Brand Step #2 and #3 and focus on a good pricing structure and lead generation.

Poor Leadership Communication

Not having a clear leadership plan can result in un-inspired team members, poor output, and faster turnover. All of these outcomes hurt a company's sustainability and will burn you out as an owner.

If we surveyed your team, would they know:

· Mission or overall goal of the company?
· Do they feel enabled to contribute to their job?
· Do they feel heard and valuable?
· Do they know that their direct report understands what they do?
· Can they define their own role and connect to how that plays a part in the greater goal of the company?

My lack of leadership is showing

My lack of leadership began to show a few years back. My team started to become unproductive and slow down on their delivery times; they also started to talk more in the office and wasted time.

That was the symptom that was presented when I neglected the importance of strong leadership. As a manager, all I was doing in the form of leadership was calling a handful of meetings, reminding the team of deadlines, and asking them for their input to make these projects better.

When I first started the business, I was looking for clones of myself to do the projects the way I would. But as our team grew, I had some incredibly talented people working with me. I needed to empower them to realize they didn't need to just fulfill what I asked them to do, but feel inspired to let their talent shine.

I encouraged them to contribute to the team in their own unique way. They were more invested in their projects. Feeling heard and valued matters!

We were able to turn things around because of this mind shift in my leadership style and crank out some amazing work to get in our production groove again.

What are you going to do to take immediate action to fix this issue?

- Is this a new leadership hire?
- Let a current team member go?
- Define and post goals for each role on the team?
- Read/listen to leadership books and other resources?
- Schedule review sessions with each team member to communicate expectations, roles, and goals?

Refer to Brand Step 4 on Team Roles to learn more.

Lack of Brand

Have you ever said this?

- "We aren't making a splash"
- "We don't stand out"
- "It's hard to explain what we do"
- "Customer ghosted us"
- "They don't pay enough attention"

Or have you heard people say this?

- "I've never heard of you guys"
- "What is it you do again?"

You'll know that you have a lack of brand and brand awareness if you don't have a good reputation with your customers and prospects. If they don't know who you are or what you care about, and can't recognize your brand in a lineup, then you have a lack of brand.

If you build it, they might get a clue

I learned to solve this problem early in my career, but I've found plenty of other speed bumps along the way. I knew building a brand was valuable when I started making a documentary for my favorite summer camp, and pitching it verbally just wasn't enough for people to understand what I was envisioning. This was a major problem because I was trying to raise donations to finish the film!

Creating a visual identity was crucial in helping build the buzz and getting others to get on board with the production. I created promotional materials like a website and movie posters so people could imagine what the film was going to look and feel like when it was done.

It was an amazing start to our fundraising campaign, along with utilizing a handful of volunteers and former camp staff to build buzz. We ended up raising enough money to finish the film and it was a centerpiece during the 50th Anniversary Gala weekend.

If you are lacking very good branding, what are you going to do to take immediate action to fix this issue?

Jump into Brand Step 1 right away and consider a refresh for your brand.

Lack of Promotion

Have you ever said this?

- "No one can find us"
- "We aren't on social media"
- "Our website is confusing"
- "Our website doesn't feel like us"
- "Our customers never hear from us"
- "We don't get enough calls"
- "We don't have anything to pass out"

Books for sale!

My wife calls me her "external hard drive" because she claims to not have a very good memory. She is wicked smart, but we tease each other about how I can remember too much and she can't remember enough. It is a fun partnership!

Because of my background in historical documentary film making and my wife's lack of memory, she and I published a book together in 2016 called *The Life & Times Annuary.*

The concept of our "Annuary" is like a diary, but for your years, rather than your days. We don't have time to write every day, but we wanted to capture our most valuable memories for the year and jot them down.

(Writer's note. I just went back to my actual Annuary to see what year we launched the Annuary because I couldn't remember! It was 2016!)

An annuary has one spread, or two facing pages, reserved for each year of your life. Every year, you add the major highlights and events so you can look back on them in the future.

The book is an amazing gift to those that use it, but the fact is no one knows it is something that they even need. It is great for genealogy groups and retirees. And it is a great gift for new babies, anniversaries, and holiday gifting.

We have not promoted this book enough, and because of that, both Jen and I moved on to more immediate money-making endeavors.

Enough about my inadequacies, if this is an issue for your company, what are you going to do to take immediate action?

- Delegate this to an ads manager?
- Create a word-of-mouth campaign?
- Make your pricing structure clearer, so people know how to buy from you?

You will be right back where you started with wasting money and resources.

If you know that Steps 1 and 2 are solid, then focus on Brand Step 3. BUT don't, I repeat, don't blow past Brand Steps 1 and 2 and skip to Step 3.

Lack of Sales Funnel

Can you track these metrics:

- Where do your leads come from?
- How many new leads do you get a month?
- What % of those leads fit your ideal customer profile?
- How many new meetings do you book a month?
- How many deals do you close a month?
- What % of customers renew each month?

Not defining your sales funnel will confuse and handcuff potential buyers from purchasing from you. You may also attract the wrong people altogether and experience issues with them once you've started to fulfill their order.

You might also not know the metrics to track to know how your business is operating. Or you might not have defined up-sell opportunities so that you can serve your customers even more than they were expecting initially.

Wham, bam, thank you, ma'am

For the longest time in my business, I worked on making the coolest project, the best art, or solving my client's concerns. I never really tracked anything except for my income and whatever project I was currently working on. A sales funnel wasn't on my radar; in fact, I didn't even know what a sales funnel was. Russell Brunson of ClickFunnels talked about McDonald's sales funnel in his books and videos.

Let's take a look at McDonald's sales funnel

Did you know that it costs McDonald's $1.91 in advertising just to get you into the drive-through, and when they sell you a burger for $2.09, they're only actually making just 18 cents, but when they up-sell you fries and a Coke for a $1.77 more, they make, and more importantly, they keep $1.32 profit. Yes, eight times the profit of the initial sale.

Without an up-sell funnel:

$1.91 advertising spend
$2.09 your spend on a burger
$0.18 profit

With an up-sell funnel:

$1.91 advertising spend
$2.09 your spend on a burger
$1.77 fries and a Coke up-sell
$1.32 profit

The power is in asking the question, "Would you like fries and a Coke with that?"

That's pretty cool, don't you think?! Okay, but what does that have to do with you?

Well, if you're like most people who sell stuff online, you've set up a website and you started to sell your product, but just like McDonald's, even if people are buying it, after your advertising costs, you're probably not left with enough to even cover your website hosting bill.

By now you must be realizing, if you want to make money online, you can't sell from a static website. You need to set up a sales funnel.

This is the sales funnel for almost every fast food restaurant out there. Starting with ordering off a menu, the customer requests items, the up-sell "ask" and then a happier customer adds more value to both the customer experience as well as the business bottom line.

Think of it as a drive-through window for your business online. Your customers are approaching your business online through a capture page. You can gather their contact information and follow up with them through email.

Then, instead of selling them a burger, you have a sales page created to sell your initial product.

This is what we call a sales funnel, where website visitors come in the top and cash comes out the bottom.

What can your "fries and a Coke" be for your business?

Your sales funnel should:

- Lead your customers through the buying process
- Offer them more of what they want
- Serve them even more in the process

What are you going to do to take immediate action to mend this issue? How can you productize your services and create up-sell opportunities to grow your sales?

Begin your work on Brand Step 2 then move on to Step 3.

Undefined Systems

Have you ever said this?

- "I have way too much work"
- "I'm not sure what each team member does"
- "It's in my email somewhere"
- "It's hard to track that"
- "I'm not sure when it's supposed to be done"
- "I don't know who's taking care of it"

Systems improve the ability to track and measure your company and allows the company to be more self-sufficient beyond needing you to be the nucleus of all the sales and operations.

If a system isn't defined clearly to you and your team, then tasks will fall through the cracks or add undue stress amongst your team. Or worse, it might be noticed by your customers, and ruin your reputation or satisfaction rate, if you were to survey your customers, sabotaging your chance to resell to those customers.

Defining your systems can be investing in software that helps you with tracking or perhaps you have the software, and you need to integrate a workflow or an automated communication system to onboard your new customers.

If you don't have proper systems in place, what can you do to get started and address this?

Growing pains

I had issues with this when I moved from being a one-man company to having team members. We lost track of our orders and where each one was in the fulfillment process. For some reason, I was trying to keep all of this information in my head. Not only was I losing track of orders, but I was also burning out and going nuts!

The solution was in creating a better system. So, I built a production tracking system and gave my entire team access to it.

This lessened my mental load, empowered my team to work autonomously, and - most importantly - got my customers their orders when they expected them.

Is this your biggest pain point?

- What are you going to do to take immediate action to mend this issue?
- How can you better define your workflow for your entire fulfillment process?
- Do you need better software?
- Do you need better integration?
- Do you need to train your team on how to follow the system?

Check into Brand Step 4 to learn more about some systems that may be helpful for your team.

Identifying Your Action Plan

Which one of these pain points is your biggest problem?

Can you pinpoint your issues and triage your business?

Take. Action. Now.

Once you've plugged the hole in your leaky boat, I want to introduce you to the Unify Brand Steps, which will save you time, money, and heartache when growing your business, but first, let me introduce myself and show you **why** these steps are so important.

Grow your company faster with this on-demand
video course led by award-winning director Bear Wade.

ENROLL TODAY:
UnifyYourMarketing.com

INTRODUCTION

*Become the general contractor
for your business marketing.*

So, you are good at what you do but are still learning how to run a successful business? This book is for you. You will have to be tenacious, organized, patient, creative, analytical, and enthusiastic to build a successful business. You can do it and I'm here to guide you through it. ((Virtual High-Five))

Sometimes, Marketing Sucks

As a business owner, you might think that marketing sucks. There's maintaining the website content, generating leads, creating a trustworthy brand, emailing your tribe, cold calling, running ads, maintaining customer satisfaction, and the total time-suck of social media. It takes time, attention, and money just to check the boxes!

It's difficult to figure out what's working and it's overwhelming to try and do it all yourself.

I've used these brand steps to guide small one-person businesses to multi-million dollar companies and everything in between. Together, we've grown their profits while making them look like top industry leaders.

The brand steps have helped me win awards, get national coverage, sell more products faster, and give business owners confidence that their company can carve out a market share in their industry. It doesn't matter if it is B2B or B2C, this process works every time.

This book was written for those of you who are ready to take your brand to the next level. If you've ever stayed up at night worried about what to do next or how to focus your energy, the five Unify Brand Steps will build your confidence and put your marketing on auto-pilot. This book will move you through the steps so that you can Define, Build, Grow, Be Top-of-Mind, and Scale your business this year.

> One Unify client (a non-profit software consulting firm) gained a 900% return on their investment using this system. Other clients crushed their sales goals and in faster times.
>
> It may seem too good to be true, but we promise it will work for you!

You'll walk away with clarity on what marketing action to take next.

This framework is something that I wish I had had when I was starting in business almost two decades ago, fresh out of college.

Over that time, I've learned that you can't build a good business solely on an idea or even a very useful product. You can make money on something and then start losing it, and even lose your investment completely.

The truth is that you have to focus on a good business model and create products and services that are measurable, repeatable, and scalable. If I had known that, then my business would have thrived sooner and my career would have felt far stabler.

My Real-Life Example

There I was sitting in my home office with my fat-faced pointer/pit mix of a dog, aka my lazy sidekick Sonic. I was trying to turn 200 hours of footage into a 2-hour film that I was hoping to get on public television.

I was a no-name videographer trying to break into TV with a documentary film made for the people - inspired, of course, by Ken Burns. *Paving the Way: The National Park-to-Park Highway* captured a 1920s road trip that traversed twelve national parks. It was badass.

Twelve adventurous people drove their Model T-looking cars across muddy, unpaved roads with no air conditioning, cellphones, maps, or perfectly distanced gas stations to hit for snacks. Can you imagine driving for 76 days over 5,000 miles in those conditions?

I knew that my documentary had a place in primetime, but I didn't know how to market or sell it.

Money was so tight that I looked down at my dog at that moment and wondered if I'd have to sell him like Sylvester Stallone sold his bullmastiff for $50 to get his script "Rocky" sold. We were living off of my wife's salary, and every penny I earned on the side was being thrown at finishing the film.

I was juggling a lot of balls to keep the whole thing going. I had to pay contractors to compose and produce original music and visual effect artists to bring some movement and dimension to the story; there was color grading and making master tapes, and I also had to pay for my fresh-out-of-college and never-written-a-script-before writer. The decision was crippling me as a sorely underpaid director, executive producer, editor, janitor, and freelance hustler.

It was scary.

But first, a joke

Do you know what the difference is between a documentary filmmaker and a large pizza? A large pizza can feed a family of four (queue to the somber orchestral music).

Being a documentary filmmaker it is hard enough to travel, manage the gear, figure out how to pay your bills, and tell a good story.

I had to figure out a way to make this thing look like I knew what I was doing, or else I would be eating Ramen, single and alone 'till my dying days.

I went to seek guidance at my local public television station in St. Louis, but they had never worked with outside producers before and couldn't take it on.

I started writing letters and tried to find a station that would help guide me through the process of getting into public television.

With every minute of not knowing my fate, the pressure continued to build. All of my friends and family knew that I was making this thing, and I had faith in my abilities to complete the film, but the success relies on people seeing it.

I can produce quality content all day long, but that doesn't mean anyone will see it and my business doesn't run very well if I don't have any eyeballs on my cool s#!t.

This isn't the *Field of Dreams*. As much as this Iowa native has the mentality of "If you build it, they will come," I knew even then that making it was just the first hurdle. I also had to find ways to promote it to the audiences who would want to see it.

Just in the nick of time (thank goodness for Sonic)... I was referred to Montana PBS. They guided me through the process of getting into the Fall Marketplace, which is like public television's very own Sundance Film Festival.

They also charged a four-figure fee to represent me and my film. To be fair they did a great job, and the people over at MTPBS are great, I'm just highlighting my financial burden.

I realized that we were going to be investing more money into this venture. I felt like I was just throwing money at my ignorance. I was in over my head and fighting way above my weight class. I was out of my league. The TV was "big boy" money and a "big boy" game.

I didn't know this at the time, but each PBS station is in charge of its own programming and each one has its own program director. And all 250 of these directors go to the Fall Marketplace and watch hundreds of submissions to see if they would be interested in carrying any of them.

To garner any interest in our program, I'd have to get over 50 votes out of 250 voters. If I did, a director might make an offer to put it in their catalog and possibly schedule it for broadcast.

Doesn't sound too reassuring, does it?

I had been doing brand work for a handful of clients to help pay for the financing of this film. As I was bootstrapping, I decided to check out what other filmmakers were doing to show off their films as professional and industry caliber. I noticed a lot of similarities in how these films were designed.

We need a captivating photo that can be used for:

- The DVD cover
- The movie poster
- Print ads
- The front of the website

I worked hard to make a film that wasn't finished looking like it was top-notch and professional, something Ken Burns and other documentary filmmakers would have produced.

I created a seamless montage of a few archival photos to use as my cover image. One of the photos was of our film's hero. I placed him near the top and I took an image of the terrain with rutted wagon paths and snow-capped mountains and blended the two together. I noticed that the back of all of the DVD cases had a short synopsis, information about the total running length, rating, stereo sound, and had a standard DVD logo.

I noticed the way the credits were ordered and formatted, and I reverse engineered mine to look like Hollywood movie credits. I knew that having light text over a dark background made things look more professional.

We went on to get 200 votes at the Fall Marketplace and *Paving The Way* was one of the key films released in the spring of 2009! I couldn't have been happier and more relieved to have made something that people still enjoy to this day.

Mr. Stallone ended up contacting the new dog owner to get his dog back once the script sold and the owner offered to sell it for $3,000 or have a part in the movie. Apparently, you can see that dude early on in the first film.

Paving The Way went on to win four Telly Awards including a documentary for television, music, writing, and cinematography.

I never got over how this kid in his late twenties with his associate's degree who managed a team of contractors could become one of the premiere films on public television that spring.

But what was the most incredible part was that I really did "fake it 'till I made it" by having really good ***branding***.

Unified branding is the key to perceived value.

This approach secured sponsorships with:

- AAA with cash and national promotion to their members
- *American Road* Magazine who traded in-video ads for print ads in their magazines
- RV America, which traded the use of one of their Class C RVs for 46 days, in exchange for a 5-second ad that we produced placed at the beginning and end of the film.

These sponsorships all came BEFORE the film was done.

We created an identity for an idea, and people understood that idea clearer and wanted to be a part of it.

To the viewers, the quality of my branding reflected the quality of my product, which then defined how serious people took me and my film. Quality branding introduces you as an industry leader, authentic to the experience they were going to have.

Most business owners have great ideas and good intentions, but their presentation just doesn't reflect the quality of their skill. This is what this book is all about.

My Back-Assward Journey Into These Steps

Over the last decade, a lot of my bread and butter work has been producing corporate films for companies around the United States. And almost every time the story plays out the same:

I'm invited to their offices and I enter into the pre-production meeting with a room full of leaders and decision-makers. We talk about the story, our target demographic, who should be cast in the video, and how this video will hook our viewers.

I tell the client that we'll have a nice clear shot of their domain name at the end of the video, which will grab new viewers and compel them to go to the website. Then I ask if their website is converting viewers into paid customers because that is the whole point of making this video: to hook people and drive action.

Most of the time their answer is something like: "Well, we have a website, but it doesn't convert viewers." We both look at each other, realizing that without a great website, making a video is kind of just throwing time, money, and resources into a void.

So we take a step back. We start talking about the idea of refreshing their website to make it clearer and feel more authentic. We talk about the flow and customer journey and start to define our major goal of having a website.

Are we trying to book meetings?

Are we trying to sell services?

Are we trying to sell products?

They need to funnel their viewers that have a certain problem to the right solution that we are offering. So, we agreed on developing their website before moving into the video.

When we meet about the website and the discussion inevitably leads to branding, a similar scenario plays out.

And so we take another step back! Ugh!

After playing out this same scenario for the last 20 years, it's become clear that there's an order to build and market a business and nobody is talking about it! If we take the right steps in the right order, we can save a bunch of time, money, and heartache.

Every year, thousands and thousands of dollars are wasted because businesses are checking off boxes, throwing sub-par websites up, forgetting they even created social media accounts, never mind creating strategies that would convert. I knew I needed to do something to help. And that is how the Unify Brand Steps came to life.

> *Businesses are throwing money away because they do things out of order.*

Imagine how fast and inexpensive it would be to make a brochure, website landing page, and short explainer video if you had this figured out already:

- Logo
- Brand elements
- Brand script
- Good photography/video of your product/service
- Testimonials
- Call-to-action

If you have these elements defined, then you can knock out cohesive and clear marketing materials by just reformatting these elements into that medium, saving you a TON of money.

Red Meat Lover

Since 2015, I've partnered with Joe Lampe of Red Meat Lover, teaching people how to cook any cut of meat with any type of heat. Think of it as a bunch of buddies bullshitting around the grill working to become better at their craft but not taking life too seriously.

We have a growing website of 50k monthly viewers, modest social media accounts, and an email database so we can notify our email subscribers every time we launch a new video recipe each week.

The main focus in our business is our YouTube channel which (as I write this) has 142 videos, 8.2 million views, 128,000 subscribers, and exponentially climbing. Ka-Chow!

Joey is the on-camera host, and I'm the one filming and photographing his recipes, experiments, and guest chefs in their own restaurants.

We have grown our team to a few video editors, social media managers, website content producers, and brand managers, all of whom are part-time contractors.

At this point, Red Meat Lover is a self-sustaining business and we are poised to become a very profitable one in the coming years.

I bring this up to reiterate that using the brand steps works!

A Brand Wake-Me-Up

Whether we like it or not, when we see forest greens and rustic browns, chances are we feel a caffeine craving comin' on. And that is what Starbucks has been working towards since the early '70s. We know their Siren logo, the comfort of their cafes, and the tribe-forming nomenclature when ordering a drink at the counter. With their font choices, color palette, photography, and decor we can walk into any shop around the world and immediately feel comfortable.

That is unifying a brand.

The 5 Unify Brand Steps are a proven framework that has worked for organizations big and small in almost any industry out there. I've worked with one-person solopreneurs and large organizations with hundreds of staff and branches around the continent.

I've been in business for the last two decades, but as I have been growing my company over the last 5 years I've realized that it takes a lot of energy and dedicated focus to create a professional and memorable brand. It can be overwhelming or easily ignored, or crazy expensive if you don't keep track of what you're doing.

It is time to realize that we have to stop making the "thing" we are good at making, and push pause. We need to be able to clearly communicate why our "thing" is so important. Then figure out how to get that message in front of the people who are having the problem our "thing" solves. Rinse. Repeat. Profit.

The whole goal of this book is to get you thinking like the general contractor of your business.

You don't have to know exactly how to do everything, like building a website, designing a logo, or producing quality ads.

You do need to know the order and specific elements that will make your marketing stand out. Your job is to lay out the blueprint and find the right team to build a high-impact professional business.

This is a workbook, I'll be leading you through exercises I've used with my clients, using a pen/paper or whatever to track and reference your progress.

There are valuable pieces in here that can inform your future marketing forever.

Come back to the 5 Unify Brand Steps often. Check off what you have done - and done well - and continue to work towards building a brand that is sustainable and profitable.

I hope you find these brand steps practical and that they act as a trusted guide as you grow your company.

 EXERCISE   UNIFY STEPS QUIZ

Not sure which Unify Brand Step you are on?

Take our FREE quiz at BearWade.com/Quiz

FOUNDATIONAL WORK

Build your marketing upon a firm foundation to protect your future investments.

Start with a solid foundation to build upon

When I was working on *Paving The Way* I told people about it all the time. I was traveling, working on this mystery movie, and everyone was intrigued. Whether at parties or events, with friends or family, everyone asked: "So, what's the movie about?"

I didn't have a good answer.

To illustrate my point, I'll share a little rendition of the tune I'd break into. (ahem)

"Uh.. well..It's a movie (duh) about these people... these friends. I guess... who drove all their old cars around together to the national parks. And, ah, there were only 12 at the time because this was in 1920... But get this...there weren't even paved roads! Or gas stations! Or GPS!"

Everyone knows that to get someone leaning into what you're doing, you need an elevator pitch. That ten-second script that makes people want to know more in just the time it takes to ride an elevator. I didn't have one. I didn't have a summary. I didn't really have in my mind a clear and concise way of saying what it was I was doing running all over the place. I also didn't have the confidence to speak to my film.

Internally, I used the excuse of "as a documentary filmmaker, I haven't discovered what the actual story is yet. I'm still crafting it" but that wasn't really true.

I did know enough about the story to share it with others, but just didn't know how. I wouldn't make eye contact when I talked about it. I looked down at my shoes.

That translated into their feelings about my film as well. Their eyes glazed over when I started mumbling.

I had to come up with a better way of explaining what it was about - something that made people want to see the dang thing! Or at least ask a follow-up question.

Sometimes I was so bad at pitching you could hear the proverbial crickets chirp after I stumbled through my pitch.

That's where my wife came in. She pointed out that we should come up with a better way to talk about the film that got people engaged. I didn't even realize how bad my version was until she helped craft our brand script.

The Brand Script

Call it a brand script or value proposition or synopsis... it's all roughly the same thing: a clear and concise set of words that have been thought out, challenged (with your team or colleagues), rearranged, swapped out, and turned into something that is very clear and memorable for both you and the listener.

A brand script uses the elements of storytelling to connect your customer (the main character) with their pain (the conflict) and how you solve their problem (with a resolution). Once you sprinkle in your credibility as an industry authority (as the author) you will give your potential customer (the reader) a compelling reason to buy from you. (So they can be the hero of their own story!)

I highly recommend Donald Miller's book *Building A Storybrand* (as well as the rest of his books) as he uses his background as an experienced author to break down how we can use storytelling in our marketing as business owners.

If you can say what you do in one compelling sentence, you hook your audience.

> ### *My New and Improved Elevator Pitch That Nobody Can Resist*
>
> *Now, when I'm at a party and someone asks about the movie, I say:*
>
> *"Paving the Way: The National Park-to-Park Highway is a historical documentary about 12 1920's motorists. Together, they drove their Model T-looking cars over 5,000 miles to all 12 of the existing national parks in 76 days.*
>
> *Before there were gas stations, air conditioning, maps, cell phones, even paved roads! Can you imagine trying to do that? Which national parks have you been to?"*

You can see that I end my pitch - that I can recite over and over - with an engaging question. I want to draw out something that might be familiar to them and get the conversation going. It gives them a place to start to engage and be part of my story.

Crafting and iterating your elevator pitch

My wife and I sat down and figured out what we needed to be included in the brand script.

We wanted to include words and phrases such as:

- "Historical documentary"
- "National parks"
- "Road trip"
- "5,000 miles"
- "Over 76 days," and
- "1920."

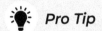

By saying "Model T-looking car", rather than "old car", we gave people a clear picture in their mind. They could envision the people and cars in the film.

Make your script easy to remember

Another significant piece to consider: it needs to be easy to remember. This is as true for you as it is for your listeners. This way you can both understand and repeat it. Sometimes you have to arrange things in an order that is easy for both you and the listener to remember.

Even after moving onto new projects, I refer to my brand script for *Paving the Way* a couple of times a month. I tell a new prospective client that I am an award-winning filmmaker to demonstrate my experience and credibile expertise. They always ask, "Really? What's the film about?" I always have my pitch in my proverbial back pocket, ready to pull out and put into people's minds.

That is one thing I love about the brand script is that you get to be a bit of an Illusionist. You create some content, some ideas, and then incept them into the mind of your listener. And then they'll be equipped to share that with their friends and colleagues when the time comes. If done right, you can live rent-free in someone else's mind for decades.

People don't buy what they don't understand

If you're always there when someone asks about your brand, why does your pitch have to be so keyed in?

First, because you need to captivate your audience. Whether that's at a cocktail party or a virtual networking event.

Second, because you shouldn't be the only one talking about what you're doing.

If you use the right words simply, it's easier for somebody to share your company or your product or service with somebody who might need it. It is perfect for sales and networking meetings. You can also put this right on your website, brochure, and social media. You can even use it as part of your script for your next video.

Our search for meaning

We will talk about this in the next chapter, but having your pitch revolve around a problem and solution is what we crave as humans.

According to molecular biologist John Medina of the University of Washington School of Medicine, the human brain craves meaning before details. When a listener doesn't understand the overarching idea being presented in a pitch, they have a hard time digesting the information.

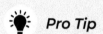

Pro Tip

Marketing is all about empathy. It's about understanding the people you want to serve, naming the challenges that keep them up at night, deeply understanding their experience, and providing a solution based on your own experience navigating those troubled waters.

50%
of your brain is utilized in visual processing

70%
of sensory receptors are in your eyes

0:01 seconds
time we take in visual stimulation

Unpacking Some Marketing Terms & Concepts

In this next section I want to break down or unpack some common marketing terms that sometimes get used interchangeably, and I'll share with you my thoughts on the differences between them, so you can think about them more clearly as you are growing your business.

Marketing vs. branding

Your vibe attracts your tribe.

There is a common misconception that marketing and branding are the same. I am guilty of using the words interchangeably. Think about it this way:

- Branding is your identity and how people feel about you.
- Marketing is what you do to reach your target audience.

Advertising vs. publicity

Advertising is what you pay for, publicity is what you pray for.

- Advertising is paying to place your marketing material in or on third-party marketing channels.
- Publicity is the free sharing of your content in other people's networks.

Is your business model even good, bro?

I'm serious. There's no reason to toil away at a business model that may not be a good one in its current form. This isn't to say that you have to start from scratch, but you might consider retooling a few things before you get too far into these Brand Steps.

Consider your business model

You might consider refreshing your business model if:

- You sell one-off products or services
- You offer too much and you carry too much inventory
- You don't offer up-sell opportunities

I realized late in the game that it was my business model that was hurting my business, and not the quality of my work. And I want nothing more than to pass on that wisdom to you so your business can thrive.

If you have an established business that you're looking to grow, complete the Unify marketing audit of your current marketing plan, below.

Asking the right questions will lead to valuable insights into your company's past, and help align your trajectory and your mindset to get the most out of the brand steps.

 EXERCISE   MARKETING AUDIT

Marketing Audit

This is our marketing audit we use when working with a new client and want to get a better understanding of where they are in the brand steps, what has worked in the past, and what they are struggling with the most.

I encourage you to fill out this guide. You can even take it online at our website, BearWade.com. It should take you 30-45 minutes to complete.

Note: We use "Client" and "Customer" interchangeably for this Audit.

Brand Messaging

Who are you? _____

_____

How are you different from others in your field? _____

_____

What does your customer need, what is their struggle? _____

_____

Why are you the best brand to help your customer? _____

_____

How can you help guide them? _____

_____

What do others (client or not) say you are? _____

_____

What do you think your clients would say about you? _____

_____

Do you have an elevator pitch? What is it?   ☐ Yes ☐ No

_____

_____

Do you have a professional logo signature in place?   ☐ Yes ☐ No

Do you have a color palette and style guide defined?   ☐ Yes ☐ No

Current Lead Acquisition Pipeline / Sales Funnel

Where do your leads come from? _____

_____

How many new leads do you get a month?_____

What % of those leads fit your ideal customer profile? _____

Do you want to find more of them or find new industries/niches to tap into?

_____

How many new meetings do you book a month? _____

How many deals do you close a month? _____

What percentage of customers renew each month? _____

Who are your most valuable clients? _____

_____

What do you know for sure has been working? _____

_____

_____

What things have you focused on to get new clients? _____

_____

What does your current workload look like? _____

_____

    How about the rest of your team? _____

    _____

What parts of your day-to-day are spent on sales/marketing? _____

_____

Sales Process

Who is your target demographic? _____

_____

Who is your bread and butter client? _____

_____

Who is your ideal client? _____

_____

What is your current sales process?_____

_____

Do you have a money-back guarantee?_____

_____

How easy is it to sign up with you?_____

_____

How hard is it to cancel with you?_____

_____

What are your pricing plans? _____

_____

_____

_____

_____

What is your current sales pitch? Why pick you? _____

_____

_____

_____

How easy is it for them to pay you? _____

_____

Do you have a value proposition?   ☐ Yes ☐ No

Have you collected testimonials from happy customers?   ☐ Yes ☐ No

Does it convey a transformation that occurred
after working with you?   ☐ Yes ☐ No

Does it have any data to highlight an ROI
when working with you?   ☐ Yes ☐ No

Current Revenue Streams

What do you sell? _____

List services/products: _____

_____

_____

_____

How much does it cost? _____

_____

Do you have tiered pricing? Entry level?   ☐ Yes ☐ No

Do you offer subscriptions or packages?   ☐ Yes ☐ No

What are you hoping to sell in the future? _____

_____

What would your dream product offering look like? _____

_____

What is your current annual revenue? _____

What is your target annual revenue? _____

Profit Margin

When was the last time you raised your rates? _____

What are your current profit margins for your services? _____

_____

What percentage of your revenue is automated? _____

What percentage of your revenue is delegated? _____

What percentage of your revenue is reoccurring? _____

How could you reduce your overhead to give you more margin? _____

_____

Connect

How do you currently connect with your clients/customers? _____

_____

How do you add value to your customer's experience outside of their personal interaction with you? _____

_____

_____

EXERCISE   MARKETING AUDIT

Advertising

How do you leverage existing customers to up-sell more to them?

_____

How have you leveraged using existing customers as a referral to their network? _____

_____

Do you have a call-to-action established? What is it? _____

_____

Do you invest in Facebook, Google ads, or any digital advertising? Which?

_____

Do you invest in print advertising? (Where, term, cost, outcome?)

_____

Systems

What software do you use to help automate what you do? _____

_____

Do you have client/customer onboarding mapped out?   ☐ Yes ☐ No

What other ways do you automate your sales process? _____

_____

In what ways do you automate your fulfillment process? _____

_____

How do you track your process? _____

How do your clients get a hold of you? (phone/email/text/i-message/booking software/website contact form, carrier pigeon/smoke signals)

_____

_____

Website

Does your website feel like your company? (authentic)   ☐ Yes ☐ No

Does your website have a clear CTA? (call-to-action)   ☐ Yes ☐ No

Can your site receive money from
customers without your attention?   ☐ Yes ☐ No

When was the last time your website had a content update?

_____

When was the last time your website had a visual update/refresh?

_____

What do you want from your website? i.e. buy your service, set up meetings,
a phone call, potential clients make contact, etc.

_____

How often are you adding blog/article/news posts? _____

Website SEO - Foundation

Do you have a Focus keyword and Keyphrase established?   ☐ Yes ☐ No

Are you using it throughout your web copy?   ☐ Yes ☐ No

Adding meta descriptions?   ☐ Yes ☐ No

Using outbound links?   ☐ Yes ☐ No

Using inbound links?   ☐ Yes ☐ No

Adding image alt attributes?   ☐ Yes ☐ No

Are you listed in Google My Business?   ☐ Yes ☐ No

Are you on Google Maps?   ☐ Yes ☐ No

Is your contact info (and map when applicable)
on your website front and center?   ☐ Yes ☐ No

EXERCISE

Summary

How did you fare?

Do you know all of the answers to these questions?

Where are the answers to your liking?

What was illuminating to you?

What needs to be addressed?

Most of these issues can be addressed by adjusting your business model, systems, and working the Unify Brand Steps.

 Download a copy of this worksheet at UnifyYourMarketing.com

Customer Journey Timeline

Another good exercise when building a firm foundation is to work on defining your customer journey. The customer journey is a step-by-step process of how your customers have gone from having a problem to becoming repeat customers. Below is an example of what this journey could look like.

What steps do potential customers take and what touchpoints can you define during each phase of the process to bring them on-board as a customer?

AWARENESS	CONSIDERATION	ACQUISITION	SERVICE	LOYALTY

STEPS

AWARENESS	CONSIDERATION	ACQUISITION	SERVICE	LOYALTY
• See digital ads on FB and Google	• Door flyers	• Orders from website	• Orders from website	• Recommends us
• tradeshow booth	• Website	• Orders from consultation	• Orders from consultation	• Leaves Google Review
• Online Research	• Face-to-face sales			• Loyalty Discounts
	• Social Media			• Releasing new features

TOUCHPOINTS

AWARENESS	CONSIDERATION	ACQUISITION	SERVICE	LOYALTY
• Google Ads	• Google Ads	• Phone	• Phone	• Phone
• Facebook Ads	• Facebook Ads	• Email	• Email	• Email
• Social Media	• Social Media	• Face-To-Face	• Website Portal	• Social Media Posts
• Referral	• Website	• User Experience		
	• Email	• Personalization		
	• Phone call			

 Download a copy of this worksheet at UnifyYourMarketing.com

Your Business Dashboard: Track Your Company Data

What gets measured gets improved.

Keeping an eye on your specific metrics of your company is imperative to growing your company. For most companies, there are so many variables to manage. Having a dashboard of your key components can keep you sane.

To do this there are some helpful metrics we want to make sure that we log now, so we can track the progress you are having when applying the brand steps.

If you don't have your systems in place yet to track this data, don't worry, we can get to it in Step 5. If you can collect this data, do it.

You'll need to have your bookkeeping in order as well as your CRM organized to achieve this, which too we'll talk about later, so don't freak out if you don't have this done. Skip over this for now and flag it for later.

Open up a spreadsheet and create a "Business Dashboard."

Here are some key metrics to collect:

- Current month and year
- Number of current customers (month, quarter, year)
- The average number of sales in revenue (month, quarter, year)
- Number of first time purchasers (FTP) acquired (month, quarter, year)
- Number of units sold (month, quarter, year)
- Number of previous customers in your database
- The number of leads vs. paid customers in your database
- Sales per product offering (month, quarter, year)
- List of top 25% of customers based on total sales
    - Identify where your largest assets and liabilities are.
        - If you can nurture the ones that are the biggest, you have the ability to grow.
        - If you lose them as a customer it will have a major effect on your revenue that you'll need to replace.

Refresh this document every month to track your progress. Add this task to your calendar after the 1ˢᵗ of each month.

The Mindset of a Business Owner

Marketing your own business sucks. It is overwhelming, time-consuming, and costly. Our proven Brand Steps will simplify your marketing process, create a clear road map, and empower you to grow your brand and look like an industry leader no matter your industry or target demographic.

As you start to scale your business, start shifting your mindset. You won't be working in the business anymore but on the business.

The goal is to build a business that can run independently, or at least still makes money without any direct effort. That is my ideal goal: to be on a beach somewhere while I'm still making vaults of money AND making a positive impact on my industry!

I am giving you permission to not do anymore "button clicking" or "lever pulling" in your business, but manage people who do that for you so you can scale your growth. You'll define which buttons and levers make your work valuable and then delegate tasks outside of your power zone to capable, well-hired team members. Then, you'll be free to have more time with your loved ones. Once you scale your business, you can be sipping Mai Tais on a tropical beach somewhere.

We are going to learn to let go and rely on finding the right people and training them using good communication and leadership skills as we move forward.

If you are worried about letting go of one aspect of your business, it is because you haven't figured out how to define how to replicate it, or you haven't found the right person to give that task to yet. Or perhaps you have tried in the past, and it crashed and burned (been there!) and now you have learned that lesson of "if you want it done right, you have to do it yourself" which is BS, because nobody would ever stay in business if they couldn't learn to lead, delegate, train and inspire.

What will make your business successful is being a leader who can communicate your expectations and empower your team to meet those expectations and use their expertise to make it better than you ever could by yourself.

Just because you are good at a trade doesn't mean you are cut-out to be a business owner or leader. But that also doesn't mean that you can't learn the skills to be a great business owner and leader. To grow your company, it is your job to execute the vision and hire the right people to pull it off.

Throughout this book, I'm going to assign what work you need to do, and what work you should consider hiring out. Don't worry, I share with you how to find and hire the right people too.

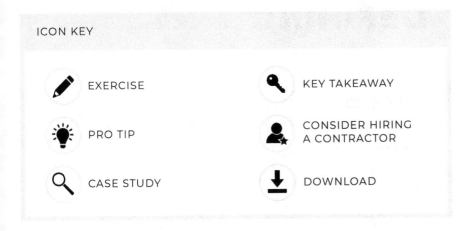

ICON KEY

EXERCISE   KEY TAKEAWAY

PRO TIP   CONSIDER HIRING A CONTRACTOR

CASE STUDY   DOWNLOAD

Do you want to build a business or just get paid for something you are good at doing?

This book can serve as your blueprint for building an actual business, and not just finding a way to sell something you are good at. There is a difference between these two ideas, that I didn't realize until I was working at it for years the wrong way.

Yes, I'm going to encourage you to invest your money in scaling your team. After reading this book, you will be able to invest in good people and work with them on getting a return on your investment. If this sounds impossible, I get it. The alternative is burnout, failure, or death. But seriously. You can do it!

People like Rockefeller, Ford, Gates, Jobs, Blakely, and Bezos didn't do it alone. They have a team that helped them scale.

Now, I'm not suggesting that you need to become one of these moguls to become successful. But before they scaled their companies, they weren't the successful entrepreneurs that we know them as today.

UNIFY STEP 1

DEFINING

Defining your brand script, brand identity, & brand media is the key to maintaining a unified brand message.

01
DEFINING

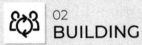
02
BUILDING

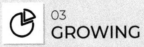
03
GROWING

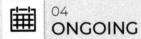
04
ONGOING

05
SCALING

CHAPTER 1

THE BRAND SCRIPT

Elements and questions to consider

People don't buy what they don't understand

The first step to Unify Your Marketing is to define who you are and get all of your marketing assets together. We'll define your value proposition, core insight, tagline, and call-to-action. From there, we work together to define your logo signature, brand colors, fonts, and additional design elements. All of these pieces make up your brand style guide and they'll be integral as we move into crafting brand photos, brand videos, and testimonials. Let's dive right in! You're in business which means you know how to solve problems. Crafting your brand script starts with defining the problem your business solves.

A brand script is a few paragraphs that walk your potential customer through why you are the solution for them.

If you can empathize with your viewers' problems you'll get their attention. Show your target audience that you have walked in their shoes.

When you share your story of how you've experienced what they're going through, they are more likely to believe that you can help them.

You craft your brand script to draw people into your story and get them to like and even love, your brand over time.

To do that, you have to identify exactly who it is you're speaking to. It can't be some nebulous customer out there in the void.

Successful brand scripts speak to their ideal customers, that person out there who is living, breathing and needing their product or service.

Niche down to move up

The first thing you need to do is niche down within your industry. You can't be all things to all people.

For example, let's say you want to start a fitness business. Great! That's always in demand. However, competition is fierce. There are countless personal trainers available online. Does this mean you can't succeed if you set out along this path? Of course not.

Rather, it means you need to get specific early and have a plan of action in terms of content creation.

With the above example, if you are setting out for a career in fitness, start niching down by asking yourself some of the following questions:

- Do I primarily want to help men, women, elders, or children?
- What type of fitness will I teach: strength training, cardio, swimming, or a specialty like dance or boxing?
- What nutrition style will I use to guide my clients - clean eating, 80/20, flexible macros?
- What makes ME unique in my field?

Once you have niched down, you then need to focus on creating and reaching your ideal client. All of this needs to be done before you even begin on your content creation journey. For your ideal client, ask yourself questions such as:

- How old is my ideal client?
- What are their interests?
- What would they be looking up online in terms of fitness (weight loss, cardio, etc)
- How can I be of value to them in their journey?
- What speaks to them?

 EXERCISE

Who Is Your Ideal Customer?

Close your eyes and imagine your ideal client. The person who is going to hear about your product gets pumped to buy it and becomes a loyal customer for a long time.

Review these questions and be specific as you answer them (with a pen and paper, or a laptop!) Keep tinkering until you have a solid understanding of who your ideal customer is. This is your ideal customer profile (ICP), customer avatar, or buyer persona.

What gender would they identify as? _____

How old are they? _____

What is the highest degree or level of school they've completed?

_____

What industry do they work in? _____

What is the size of their organization? (B2B applicable)

_____

What is their job title? _____

How is their job measured? (Leads generated, revenue generated, team productivity, etc.) _____

_____

Who do they report to? _____

_____

What are their goals or objectives? _____

_____

_____

What are their biggest challenges? _____

_____

_____

What are their job responsibilities? _____

_____

_____

What tools do they use or need to do their job? _____

_____

_____

How do they prefer to communicate with vendors or other businesses?

☐ Phone

☐ Email

☐ Text Messaging

☐ Social Media

☐ Face-To-Face

How do they gain information?

☐ Online courses

☐ Conferences

☐ Email newsletters

☐ Websites

☐ Trade Magazines

☐ Social media

☐ Other _____

What social media networks do they belong to?

☐ Facebook

☐ Instagram

☐ Twitter

☐ Clubhouse

☐ LinkedIn

☐ Pinterest

☐ Other _____

 Download a copy of this worksheet at UnifyYourMarketing.com

Steve Johnson

42
Des Moines, IA
Business Owner
Married, two girls (Clara 12 & Hope 10)

Favorite Brands

Bio

Steve owns a CPA firm in Grimes, IA. He has 2 other business partners and 4 other associates and is just starting an internship program at his firm. He has an office, has steady clients and enjoys time with his family. Originally from Twin Cities, he played baseball in high school and college at Drake. He enjoys BBQing, fishing, and hunting in the summer and fall when he isn't involved with his church and his family.

Wants & Needs

Because his work is seasonal, he is always looking for new income streams and ways to market his firm outside of the tax season. He is getting more corporate accounts but needs to step up his firm's marketing if he wants to compete with the bigger firms in Des Moines.

Frustrations

Steve has trouble finding time to manage his marketing day-to-day. He doesn't have time to keep up with his firm's social media and isn't sure where to start.

Here you can see we took it a step further and mocked up a whole ideal customer persona. All of this is completely made up but is a lot like the types of people we want to target in our marketing.

Define Your Value Proposition

So, let's talk about why anyone should pick you over the competition. This is where you need to be ruthless with what makes you valuable.

This value proposition isn't about your worth, nor the expense your business has taken on. It is about articulating your product or service's value to the potential customer.

In Russell Brunson's book, *Traffic Secrets*, he says that people buy things because of three motivations: health, wealth, or relationships.

So, which one of those three categories most resonates with the outcome of your customer's experience?

Here are 5 ways to think about how to communicate your value:

- Identify all the benefits your product offers.
- Describe what makes these benefits valuable.
- Identify your customer's main problem.

- Connect this value to your buyer's problem.
- Differentiate yourself as the preferred provider of this value.

Here is an example of what a brand script could look like for a grocery delivery service business:

You don't have to waste time and money by going to the grocery store. Between driving to and from the store, navigating the isles, negotiating with your kids, buying extras that catch your eye, and carrying heavy loads to your car, it can take away valuable family time and bloat the budget and waistline. And we believe there is a better way. All you have to do is download our app, shop online, reduce the temptations while maintaining healthy decisions, and your groceries appear at your kitchen counter within hours.

Every good brand script:

- Starts with a problem
- Highlights your ideal customer's struggles
- Shows the negative consequence your viewer might have if they don't use your product or service

Creating Your Brand Script

To create your brand script, let's ask good questions and come up with clear answers. So, grab a pen and paper, and let's jot down some ideas here:

Question 1: What is a negative consequence if they don't use your product or service?

We want you to articulate what your potential customer will be like (or still be like) if they don't buy from you.

Here are a handful of examples:

- If they don't use your car tires, they might slip off the road, get hurt or worse!
- If they don't use your toothpaste, you won't have that white smile, be as attractive, get attention.
- If they don't use your home cleaning service, they'll have to spend all weekend doing chores instead of enjoying family time outside!

Here is one from my company:

If you don't use the five Brand Steps you won't look very professional or legitimate, or like you have your s*** together and people won't value your business, product, or service. You'll continue to feel overwhelmed as a business owner or confused about what to do next in your marketing and you will waste time and money.

Another example could come straight from Paving The Way:

If you had a car in 1920, you likely struggled to drive it around town. Roads were unpaved, muddy, rutted, and unmarked.

And because there were no paved roads, no good maps, gas stations, signage, or air conditioning, you likely didn't take it beyond the city limits.

Question 2: What is a common misconception in your industry? Where has the industry stopped growing and improving? How have you innovated?

Point out a standard way of doing business that can be improved or you can talk about your values and why your customers can be released from the burden of this problem.

Once you reveal the misconception and grab your audience's attention, you then proclaim what you stand for. How can you make lives easier? What motivates you to be in business? What is just plain wrong about your industry that needs to change through your solution?

For example:

A common misconception is that it is cheaper to do your marketing. Rather than bearing the weight of needing to do it all your own, it is more cost-effective in the long run to hire Unify Creative Agency to guide you through the marketing process in order so you can do it once and do it right.

Another example could come straight from Paving The Way:

Until 1920, you didn't even consider driving your car outside city limits. It was just a fun and less smelly tool to get you from point A to B substituting your need for a horse and carriage.

Question 3: What does success look like?

List the positive change your customers will experience if they use your product or service.

We want to show them what it feels like to win— when they buy from you. Show them what it feels like when they reach the result, what success looks like.

For example, if you are using the Brand Steps:

With the Brand Steps, you'll have a marketing game plan, clarity on what to focus on, know their next steps, feel empowered, smart, and capable.

Another example could come straight from Paving The Way:

12 motorists drove 5,000 miles over 76 days to all 12 of the national parks on one continuous muddy trail.

After the Park-To-Park Highway Tour, more Americans decided to stay and "See America First" and not travel back to Europe for holiday. They didn't have to succumb to the schedule and expense of the train. They were in control. And seeing many of the National Parks was as spectacular as any sight abroad.

Question 4: What is your three-step process?

What three steps does your ideal customer need to take to start working with you?

You want to make these three steps so clear that your ideal customer naturally commits to working with you or buying your product.

If someone has to hunt for how to reach out to you or what you offer in the way of bundles or products, you're putting more obstacles in their way of buying from you. Spell it out very simply so they can take action quickly.

For example:

1. *Go to BearWade.com*
2. *Take the Brand Quiz and figure out what step you're on.*
3. *Learn which solution will work best for you.*

Another example could come straight from PTW:

1. *Go to PavingTheWay.com*
2. *Rent or Purchase the film.*
3. *Take this amazing adventure.*

Question 5: What is your direct call-to-action?

A call-to-action is saying what action your reader needs to take to move forward with you.

Do they need to:

- Visit your website?
- Click on the link below?
- Give us a call?
- Book a discovery call?
- Sign-up now!

Define the call-to-action and then use it everywhere, so we don't confuse the viewer with options that might lead to not acting at all.

This should be noted in the form of a button on your website, by bolding it or using a highlight color to catch our viewer's attention. We want to direct them into your sales funnel, which we'll talk about later.

For example: Go to BearWade.com and take the brand quiz.

Another example could come straight from PTW: Watch at PavingTheWay.TV

Put it all together

Now let's put it all together, starting with the problem and ending with the direct call-to-action.

The Bear Wade script could be this:

As a business owner managing your own marketing can be overwhelming, a waste of time and money, or it gets ignored.

It is a common misconception that it is cheaper to do your own marketing and bear the weight of doing it all yourself as a business owner. However, by not investing in the experts and misplacing your energy and expertise, you actually sabotage your marketing efforts.

Bear Wade guides you through the process of discovering which brand step you are on, empowering you with a solid game plan on what to focus on when creating your brand.

Take the Unify Brand Steps quiz at BearWade.com to discover which brand step you are on, today!

The Paving The Way script sounds like this:

If you had a car in 1920, you likely struggled to drive it out of town. Roads were unpaved, muddy, rutted, and unmarked.

And because there were no paved roads, no good maps, gas stations, signage, or air conditioning, most people didn't even consider driving their car outside city limits. It was just a fun and a less smelly way to get you from A to B within town, (no horse manure to worry about and you didn't have to rely on someone latching up your carriage!)

This is why it is so incredible that 12 intrepid motorists drove their new cars over 5,000 miles in 76 days to all 12 of the national parks on the newly named Park-To-Park Highway, an unpaved, unsigned, muddy trail that connected the parks.

As a result of the Park-To-Park Highway Tour, more Americans decided to cancel their European holiday to "See America First". They didn't have to succumb to the schedule and expense of the train. They were in control. And seeing many of the National Parks was as spectacular as any sight abroad.

Go to PavingTheWay.com to rent or purchase the film and travel alongside in this amazing adventure, today!

Ramp up your confidence

The more confident and enthusiastic you present yourself, the more people will listen to what you're saying. They'll lean in and reflect your energy back to you.

"Your Excitement + Their Doubt = Their Intrigue"

RYAN DIESS

People engage with confident people. They believe that what you have to say is something worth listening to and they become more engaged. They ask follow-up questions and make their way down closer towards the point of purchase. Even if they aren't your ideal customer, they're more likely to refer you to one of their friends or colleagues.

Your vibe attracts your tribe, so practice your brand script over and over to yourself, aloud, to colleagues, and to customers.

It can be awkward at first to talk about yourself or your business. It feels like self-promotion and self-indulgence. It helps to be prepared with some talking points and even to practice with a safe audience or in the mirror.

Talk about:

· What you do
· Why you care
· Why they should care
· How you can help them
· What they should do next

Now go forth and plaster that brand script everywhere—the front of your website, your social media, print materials, press releases, everywhere you can think of! Remember, this isn't about you, but the people you are helping! Let their cries for help guide your efforts and get excited to share it far and wide.

CHAPTER 1

KEY TAKEAWAYS

Craft your brand script

- Identify your ideal customer
- Write your value proposition

  Guiding questions:

  Question 1: What is a negative consequence if you don't use our product or service?

  Question 2: What is a common misconception in your industry? Where has the industry stopped growing and improving? How have you innovated?

  Question 3: What does success look like?

  Question 4: What is your three-step process?

  Question 5: What is your direct call-to-action?

  Put it all together and you have your brand script

- Be confident in your offer!

CHAPTER 2

BRAND IDENTITY

Understanding the power of your company name, logo signatures, file types, color theory, brand colors, and having a style guide, so you can grow your brand but keep it consistent.

"Attention is the single most important asset."
– Gary Vaynerchuk

 CONSIDER HIRING A CONTRACTOR

Who Are You, Anyway?

If you read the intro, you know that your brand identity is more than just your logo. Although it's true that having a clear and simple logo that has a styled font will go a long way in branding your company, you must define your company more than that.

You won't always need or want to use your whole logo and this is why having a cohesive brand identity will make sure that you're recognizable even without it. Define your logo signature, brand colors, brand fonts, and other design elements to communicate the look and feel of who you are.

According to a Lucidpress article, there is an average increase of 33% in revenue because the brand consistently presented itself.

80% of people remember what they see, compared to 10% of what they hear and 20% of what they read.

Make people SEE what it is you do.

Your company name

While you already have a company name, don't skip over this section. Even if it requires a rebrand, it will be worth it if it is confusing, hard to remember, or stale. Your company name needs to be easy to understand, memorable, and universal. If people can't pronounce it, spell it, or understand it over the phone, chances are it isn't "sticky" enough to be memorable.

Survey people that are your ideal customers, and see if they have an opinion about your company name. See if they can remember it, know what it is about, spell it without being told. These are key indicators that you have a good name to build a brand upon.

Although, I am by no means a lawyer or CPA, in many cases the legality of changing your business name is as little as filing a "DBA" or "Doing Business As" form, and from there you can operate as the new brand name to the public.

 Pro Tip

Gather a group of peers, colleagues, friends, or what I refer to as "Trusted Advisors" that you can lean on to survey and bounce ideas off of. These people should not just be people that you pay, but also people that pay you, or might not be a paying customer yet. Define your advisors and let them know that you would love their feedback as you are building things. Just make sure you don't burn them out or overstay your welcome.

There is nothing wrong with rebranding your company if you come up with a better solution. Yes, it will take some upfront investment to change things over, but in the long run, having a name that people can remember, makes your branding efforts *so much more valuable and cost-effective.*

Common brand name no-nos

Stay away from acronyms or other codes in your name. A lot of my clients have had names that no longer represent what they do. At one time it might have made sense; other times, it was confusing from the very beginning.

When receiving feedback, keep your ears, mind, and heart open. Keep your guard down and be mindful of what they are trying to communicate to you.

Listen to what they have to say and give them space when they pause to gather their thoughts. They may have never been able to say your name correctly or even remember it let alone spell it. They may be able to do all of those things, but honestly have no idea why you chose it and how it relates to the work you do.

A time I named my business poorly:

Here is an example of when I named a business without surveying advisors. I was working in the cycling industry for about 15 years working as a contracted creative director for an event company that put on some of the world's largest cycling rides. I wanted to niche down and focus only on the cycling market and so I rebranded my company name to "Preme Brands."

Not sure how to pronounce "Preme?" Well, in my mind, it rhymes with "cream." I wanted it to sound phonetically short for Premium. But about 90% of the time people pronounce it "Pree-mie", like a baby that was born early.

In the cycling race world, the term Prime (but pronounced "preem") is a prize you can win during a stage of a race. Anyway, it didn't work, even with people in the cycling industry! (FAIL!)

I thought I could be like the person who invented the word "Swiffer." but all for not.

I did my best to educate my audience about how to say "Preme rhymes with cream" but WTH? It took a lot of energy on my part and I was confusing my audience and it was getting in the way of making sales.

How to know if you have a good brand name

If it is a good fit, then own it and run with it. But doing your due diligence now can save you a lot of heartaches later.

If you decide to rebrand, run a brainstorming session and write a couple of dozen name ideas out first. Cross off anything that doesn't resonate or fit what you do, and narrow down what feels best.

Remember: A brand name has to be easy to spell, say, read and hear. So make sure it passes all those tests before committing to something. Keep it simple and keep it memorable.

Logo Signatures

The same goes for a logo signature which is the combination of an icon with a clear typeface of the name of your company. In your signature, you can leave out the LLC or LTD (or whatever your tax classification is) and keep it to the company name itself.

Common logo signature examples..

Fonts matter

Before we get into fonts, I just want to mention the concept of a "word mark" which is a styled font that is used for your company logo and picking the right font can convey so much about your company. Choosing your font is more than choosing something that looks cool or trendy. Your font communicates who you are and what it's like to work with you.

i will always
find you

I will always
find you

Common word marks that use serif fonts.

Common word marks that use sans-serif fonts.

Classic, trustworthy, ageless = serifs

Serifs are those little elements on the end of the letters that make it feel more classic like a Times New Roman font.

Some of my favorite serif fonts are:

1. Merriweather
2. Georgia
3. Garamond

Modern, contemporary, new, and fresh = sans-serifs

These are fonts sans (or without) serifs, like Arial or Helvetica.

Some of my favorite Sans serif fonts are:

1. Helvetica
2. Futura
3. Montserrat
4. BEBAS

Icons and Emblems: Social, T-Shirts, and Other Swag

Icons or emblems, represent your brand in tight spaces. Think of social media profile photos, letterhead, or T-shirts. They're simple and easily recognizable. Some great examples are the Nike Swoosh, Apple's Apple, or Shell Gas Station's Shell. Whether we like these brands or not, these icons are very recognizable.

Rule 1: Simple is better.

You want your icon to be so simple that a kid could draw it from memory. Another good goal is to have a logo simple enough that it could be embroidered.

Rule 2: Does it pass the Black and White test?

Take a look at the two lions on the next page. Same lion, but it renders completely differently. One is fierce, steadfast, confident in his power. The other... not quite that. It looks cross-eyed! Isn't that hilarious? My kids thought so!

This logo did not pass the black and white test. Create your logo in black and white first and then ensure the logo can be reversed and still communicate the same messaging.

Yes, you can add 3D effects and outlines and drop shadows and other design features to make your logo look developed, but if it doesn't pass the black and white test continue working it until it does.

What works on white might not work reversed out, so make sure your emblem passes the test and doesn't leave you cross-eyed.

Non-Negotiable Logo Versions

Please, please, please: Do not go to all the trouble of designing a logo and then drop the ball when it comes to making it available for use.

When the talented designer you hired completes your logo and you sign off on the final, glorious piece, make sure to request both ***raster and vector*** versions of your logo.

Raster files

Raster versions are great for screen use and are usually measured in dots per inch or DPI. At its core, the term raster means that if you take a small photograph and enlarge it, it will become more and more pixelated – i.e. blurry – until it reaches the point where it is unrecognizable. As such, they don't look very good when scaled up to much larger than the original design. Other times, you are stuck with a white box around them like you see in a lot of JPG logos. No bueno.

The best raster file type is a PNG with a transparent background. PNG (pronounced PEE-en-JEE) stands for Portable Network Graphic, and it is the most frequently used uncompressed raster image format on the internet. A PNG is used for web page navigation

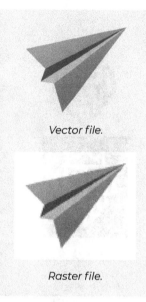

Vector file.

Raster file.

elements, graphics, and any type of image with sharp edges. In short, wherever transparency, good compression, details, and clear boundaries of the image are necessary. Make sure you're able to get a true PNG with a transparent background.

A JPG (or JPEG) stands for Joint Photographic Group and is a raster format often used for photographs on the web. JPG files are web-friendly because the files are typically smaller in file size.

The downside to JPGs is that the original quality of the image is decreased as it is compressed to keep the image size small. JPGs become blurry when used for high-quality printing. Benefits of JPGs include: they have a small file size, are compatible with almost all devices and software, and high-resolution JPEG images are vibrant and colorful.

Within the past couple of years, a new file format has become more prevalent called WebP. This format provides superior lossless and lossy compression for images on the web. Using WebP, webmasters and web developers can create smaller, richer images that make the web faster. For comparison, WebP lossless images are 26% smaller in size compared to PNGs while still supporting transparency. I imagine this file format is going to become more and more prevalent in the next few years.

The checkerboard denotes a transparent background.

Vector files

The #1 file type you need for your logo is a Vector File. Vector files are images that are built by mathematical formulas that establish points on a grid. This means they can infinitely scale in size without losing resolution-making vector files more versatile for certain types of tasks than raster files.

Common Vector file extensions are:

- **.ai** (Adobe Illustrator)
- **.eps** Encapsulated PostScript (older filetype that doesn't support transparency the same way .ai files do)
- **.pdf** (Portable Document Format)
- **.svg** (Scalable Vector Graphics)

If you were ever going to print your logo on a large scale, it is imperative to have a vector file. If you're having a designer create a logo for you or you're creating a logo for yourself, you MUST have a vector file to protect your brand in the long run to future proof your investment.

You can always turn a vector version into a raster version, but it is much harder the other way around. Asking your designer to send you a vector format of your logo is standard practice and make sure you keep the file somewhere easy to access for you to send out whenever necessary. Every designer you work with in the future - from media outlets to partners - is also going to want a vector version of your logo.

 Pro Tip

Double-check with your designer that they "outline fonts and strokes" in your vector files. Converting outlines and strokes guarantees that when you work with anyone else, whether or not they have the right fonts downloaded on their computers, your artwork will look exactly as meticulously designed.

Brand Colors

According to a study from the University of Loyola, color increases brand recognition by up to 80%. Yaow! That is something to not take lightly.

Your brand color palette is used for your logo, signature, and any branding materials including, but not limited to, your website, brochures, social media posts, and ads in videos.

Define two to five colors max and know what their color codes are for print and screen.

Color theory

Knowing just a little bit of color theory can go a long way when defining your brand colors. So let's dig into that a little bit.

The colors you choose tell the story.

Color theory for brand colors:

- *Yellow evokes clarity, warmth, and optimism.*

- *Orange evokes cheerful, confident, friendly.*

- *Red evokes bold, useful, excitement*

- *Purple evokes imaginative, wise, creative*

- *Blue evokes trust, dependable, strength*

- *Green evokes health, growth, peaceful*

- *Gray evokes calm, neutral, balance*

- *Rainbow evokes diversity, multifaceted, all-encompassing*

According to Design Buddy, 1/3 of the world's top 100 brands include the color blue in their logos.

So who are you? How do you want your customers to feel when they see your brand or visit your website?

Color Spaces

We don't need to dive too deep into color spaces, mostly because we leave that for the trained professionals. Which, if I haven't mentioned it, you should be investing in your design work.

Color spaces are a way to describe and measure color values, so we can keep colors looking consistent from device to device, computer to computer, digital to print.

The reason you should care about color space at all is that you get a better understanding of why something doesn't look right when you see it on a screen vs. printed on your home printer vs. printed on a thousand brochures by a printing press.

If you hold a printout next to your screen, it won't match for a handful of reasons. Such as: how calibrated your monitor is or what temperature of light is bouncing onto the piece of paper. If you have warm tungsten desk lamps pointing at it your colored paper will look different than if you held it under white-almost-green fluorescent light. So, just remember that as you are choosing your brand colors.

For example, Pepsi uses red and blue in their brand colors, and that red and blue look the same on their can, as on their vending machine, TV commercials, and on print ads, so defining these colors once can influence the design process throughout.

The four kinds of color languages that you should know: RGB, CMYK, HEX, and Pantone.

There is nothing more infuriating than getting a box of 1000 postcards in the mail from your printer with

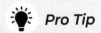 *Pro Tip*

When I choose brand colors for a client, I love to sample colors from their building interior or exterior, from their environment, or from the product itself so consider that when you are defining your brand colors.

colors that look nothing like you expected. The consolation is that you have a supply of 1000 coasters to protect your wood table from your iced tea. And, just as useful, something sturdy to fold in half and wedge under a wobbly table at your local dive bar.

Rest assured that most of the time the printing press will send you a proof for your approval. Make sure you get a good look at it *in person* before signing off on moving ahead with the full print run.

The Primary Color Spaces You Need to Know

RGB (red, green, and blue)

Uses: RGB is what we see on every screen in the world including digital devices and home printers.

RGB is denoted by a single number for each amount of Red, Green, and Blue. (37,95,145)

CMYK (cyan, magenta, yellow, and black)

(Because B was taken already for Blue)

Uses: CMYK is the "color space" that printing presses use. So, if you are having posters or brochures printed by a press, or if you are going to run an ad in a magazine or local newspaper, then you'll want to make sure that your design is in the CMYK color space.

CMYK is denoted by a single number for each amount of Cyan, Magenta, Yellow, and Black. (91,64,20,4)

HEX

Hex codes are becoming the go-to way to keep your colors consistent in the consumer space. They're denoted by using the "#" symbol and then a combination of six numbers and letters.

Hex codes are denoted by a combination of numbers and numbers. (#255f91)

Pantone (or PMS)

Uses: Printing press and clothes printing.

Pantone is a universal standard color code so that the color on one type of material matches that color on a different type of material.

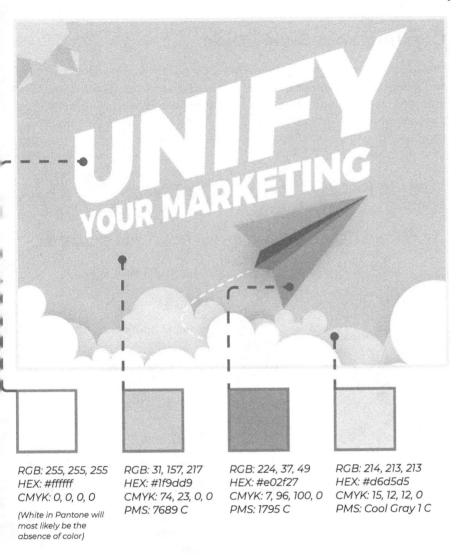

RGB: 255, 255, 255
HEX: #ffffff
CMYK: 0, 0, 0, 0
(White in Pantone will
most likely be the
absence of color)

RGB: 31, 157, 217
HEX: #1f9dd9
CMYK: 74, 23, 0, 0
PMS: 7689 C

RGB: 224, 37, 49
HEX: #e02f27
CMYK: 7, 96, 100, 0
PMS: 1795 C

RGB: 214, 213, 213
HEX: #d6d5d5
CMYK: 15, 12, 12, 0
PMS: Cool Gray 1 C

Defining Your Color Palette

If you're just starting in defining a color palette I recommend looking at what other color palettes are out there for brands that you want to be associated with.

You can reference places like Pinterest, Magazines, Websites, TV Commercials, etc. Keep a collection of your favorite color combinations. If you don't use them now for your overall brand, they might work for an upcoming campaign initiative, which we'll talk about later in Brand Step #3.

And if all else fails keep it pretty neutral and add one splash of color.

Creating Your Style Guide

Once you have your color pallet defined then you can iterate on your logo and materials with different combinations of those colors. By having at least four, you have flexibility in how you want to present yourself in certain ad campaigns, seasons, or materials. Stay organized! Create a folder on your computer that has two folders inside of it. One that says "for print" the one that says "for screen."

FOR SCREEN · PNG Files with Transparent BACKGROUNDS · RGB

HORIZONTAL LOGO SIGNATURE
- [ ] FULL COLOR
- [ ] MAIN BRAND COLOR
- [ ] BLACK
- [ ] WHITE

VERTICAL LOGO SIGNATURE
- [ ] FULL COLOR
- [ ] MAIN BRAND COLOR
- [ ] BLACK
- [ ] WHITE

EMBLEM ONLY
- [ ] FULL COLOR
- [ ] MAIN BRAND COLOR
- [ ] BLACK
- [ ] WHITE

MY BRAND FONTS ARE:

_____

_____

_____

_____

FOR PRINT · EPS Files · CMYK

HORIZONTAL LOGO SIGNATURE
- [ ] FULL COLOR
- [ ] MAIN BRAND COLOR
- [ ] BLACK
- [ ] WHITE

VERTICAL LOGO SIGNATURE
- [ ] FULL COLOR
- [ ] MAIN BRAND COLOR
- [ ] BLACK
- [ ] WHITE

EMBLEM ONLY
- [ ] FULL COLOR
- [ ] MAIN BRAND COLOR
- [ ] BLACK
- [ ] WHITE

MY BRAND COLOR CODES ARE:

_____

_____

_____

_____

Use this list as a checklist with your logo designer. You should have all of these versions of your logo clearly labeled and easy to access for marketing materials.

 Download a copy of this resource at UnifyYourMarketing.com

Style guide

Having these easily accessible will make your life way easier when promoting your business. In those folders, you should also include a style guide that can help designers, co-workers, and collaborators accurately represent you.

This style guide PDF document would show:

· Your icon

· Logo signature

· Color codes for your brand colors

· Fonts that you use

· Any additional elements that are approved to use to keep your brand messaging consistent

In this folder, you might also add your hero images, and additional key brand images formatted as big (for printing) and small (for screen) versions.

For the big versions, have them as big as you can. 5000px wide or more. And for small versions, 2000px wide is still pretty big, but you can use it for any size screen and it will still look sharp.

So when you have a trade show booth design you can use these colors and logos and fonts, and when you hire a video producer to make social media video ads they can use the same colors and fonts and logos making it all look cohesive, or dare I say... Unified! Doesn't that feel amazing?

BEAR WADE

BEARWADE.COM

Primary Colors	Secondary Colors		Icon / Favicon

255F91   F7C616   2FABF7

Primary Logo

 BEAR WADE

Please Note: Full color logo should be used at all times unless black and white is required.

Minimum Size
Bear Wade logo should be used no smaller than 1.25" wide.

 BEAR WADE
1.25"

Clear Space

Always maintain clear space around the logo to protect from distracting graphics or typography. For the logo, measure clear space by the height and width of the "B" in the Bear Wade logo.

 BEAR WADE

Alternate Logos

 BEAR WADE    BEAR WADE

BEAR WADE

Wordmark

BEAR WADE

Additional Design Elements

Typography

Headline Font Muller ExtraBold DEMO

Body Text - Open Sans Regular
14.4 pt line spacing, 0 kirning.
ABCDEFGHIJKLMNOPQRSTUVWXYZ
abcdefghijklmnopqrstuvqxyz
123456789!?#%$

Web Safe Fonts

**Headline Font: MONSERRAT
Weight 800 Size 2.5 #3C3C3C**

Body Text: Monserrat
Weight 400 Size 1.25 #3C3C3C

Bear Wade Brand Standards 2021© for more information please contact:
Bear Wade | bear@unify-agency.com

Anytime that I work with a graphic designer, website developer, videographer, or video editor, I give them this style guide which is included with my brand files, which guides them in how to use our brand and keep it constant across all mediums.

CHAPTER 2

KEY TAKEAWAYS

Solidify your brand identity

- Company name
- Logo
- Brand colors
- Color theory
- Creating your style guide
- Create folders with your must-have file types for your logo

CHAPTER 3

BRAND MEDIA

Brand media is authentic photographs, videos, and testimonials.

CONSIDER HIRING A CONTRACTOR

A common misstep is to just use whatever photos you can find that you like or that your customers might like. While you can certainly do that and slap your logo on it, defining your brand media should be far more calculated and tested. When it is, you build brand equity that is far deeper and more meaningful.

Authentic Photography

We want to define clear authentic photography of your product or service as well as mockup the customer's outcome of working with you. If you're a spa, your customers would look relaxed and their faces would be soft. If you're solving business problems, they may look excited, rich, and successful.

They say a photo can speak a thousand words, so make sure those words are clear, concise, and set the mood that you're looking for. You don't need a hundred photos to use, either. Having 5-10 top picks goes a long way and with repetition, you gain brand equity. Always hire a professional to take photos for you. Make sure they focus on quality lighting, tone, and texture.

If you are taking photos of a person, find a portrait photographer. If you are taking pictures of a product, find a product photographer.

You don't usually need a documentary session to capture good brand photos. You need a session that can be staged and controlled in the right setting.

And also in your brand photography, you can tell a story with what kind of photos you choose.

- Wide shot of your product or service in an environment.
- Mid shot with people using your product or service.
- Close-up of your product or service and maybe even an
- Ultra close-up to show off texture or a detail that you want to highlight.

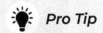 *Pro Tip*

No two photographers are the same and just because somebody has a camera doesn't mean they will show off your product or service clearly.

 Pro Tip

Shoot loose. Leave lots of room around the subject of your composition so that you can add text and your logo later. Many times photographers will crop in too tight. Cameras have such a high-resolution sensor that is easier to crop in later than it is to photoshop in more background or surroundings, so shoot loose.

This shot of Jason Pride was taken in my home office against my blackout curtains, using a softbox off-camera flash. I sat down on a chair so I would be looking up at him as if I was in the crowd. I then cut him out in Photoshop and put a blurred-out set of colors behind him and a black gradient in front of him so that we wouldn't see his jeans and could fade to black on the website, which made a nice spot for logos. Sure you might think it was taken while he was public speaking at a seminar, but no.

This photo is stock photography taken by a reputable media company. Purchasing the rights to use this was much cheaper than hiring a professional photographer to go to the beach at the right time of year and casting the perfect couple to walk hand-in-hand. There is enough room to put our hook of "How do you know when you can retire?" in the sky. But the photographer didn't shoot loose enough, (meaning they cropped too tight in-camera) so I had to Photoshop more beach, water, and sky with clouds to make it work.

Composition matters

Notice the visual balance between the people walking on the left third of the image and the content on the right two-thirds. The people are directing their eyes to where we want our viewers' eyes to go, too: the CTA! Cha-ching!

Can you see the hierarchy established here? Notice the sizing, biggest to smallest, top to bottom. See the hook at the top? Then the details near the lower third, and a solution (which is the CTA) near the bottom. These elements are laid out in a ratio of size with the priority biggest and at the top, because we read top to bottom.

I usually mock up one of these brand ads just to bring all of the elements together into one spot. I have the hero image, logo, CTA, brand script, product image, and brand colors. Now, this might change over time, but if you establish the overall design, it is easier to adjust the aspect ratio or dimensions of what you need it for.

When you're producing something like this, make it count. This ad could be utilized for social media, the website header, email campaigns, a magazine ad, and a postcard mailer. This saves you money and also makes the image sticky in the audience's mind.

Hero image

Now your turn. Your Hero image should bring all of these branding elements together. You'll be surprised at how far you've come and how many times you can come back to this file and update one element, like the hero image, or the product you are featuring, and then you have a whole new campaign message. We'll talk more about this in Brand Step #3 with Campaign Initiatives.

Brand Video: Aaaand Action! (Finally)

68% of marketers say video has a better return on investment than Google Ads.

With all of these elements established, you're ready to design your first video.

If you can, hire a videographer, who can take the technical burden off of you, because video is full of technology, theory, and can, if done well, overwhelm someone who isn't used to working with video equipment day in and day out. And this goes for editing as well.

Trends are changing with video, and social media, and YouTube has brought the average level of production WAY down, which is good and bad.

The bad: it is harder to stand out amongst all of the video content being published, which is 500 hours every minute!

The good: you don't have to be Spielberg to make good content anymore! We are seeing more and more incredible content creators every day and video is an AMAZING tool to reach your audience.

If hiring a videographer is too expensive then at least consider hiring out your editing. There are places (cough: UnifyMyVideos.com) where you can upload your raw footage and we will take it and edit it for you. This can save a TON of time in front of a computer when you should be working on creating content, not editing it.

Your brand video will be embedded within the landing page of your website. It is a quick overview of essentially your brand script and will start to humanize your brand and make your buying process easier to understand for the viewer.

You want to highlight the problem that your viewers have, then show off your solution, the process of buying your solution, and a direct call-to-action. Humor goes a long way in keeping people's attention. But if nothing else, be clear and concise. Using music and motion will go a long way as well as making your video entertaining.

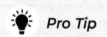 **Pro Tip**

Injecting humor into your video isn't always applicable, but it is a great way to keep people's attention and keep them engaged.

A good brand video is:

- Educational
- Entertaining
- Humorous

HubSpot reports that 78% of people watch online videos every week, and 55% view online videos every day, proving that video is a valuable tool to reach people where they are.

Casting

When casting your video, whether voiceover or on-camera talent, ***don't default to using the owner of the company as the face of the video.***

If you have employees or can hire a professional on-camera person, it's worth pursuing. Because the whole goal is to be clear and concise, sometimes the business owner isn't the right person for the job (although I'm sure you would be excellent narrators!) If you have the chance to use a diverse group to help communicate your story, that sometimes is the best way to accomplish an entertaining video.

Outline

A quality video begins with a quality outline. Define your filming location, cast, props, wardrobe, and any other elements DAYS before you shoot.

Lighting and audio

The clarity of your picture and sound matters. You want people focused on your message rather than distracted by a grainy visual or background clicking. Lighting and clear audio are more important than the camera you use if you can believe it?! We, as a society, are much more forgiving of a bad picture than we are of bad audio.

An obvious example of our tolerance of poor video and audio being a necessity is that we can use a cell phone with audio-only but we can't do Zoom on mute. People freak out, right?! Dude, you are on mute!

Our cell phones have good enough cameras to be clear, but only under great lighting, especially inside.

Why not then go outside, you ask? Well, because of noise pollution. Unwanted background noise can sabotage a good video.

Now there is a nightmare of an example, if I've ever seen one! Watch your backgrounds!

 Pro Tip

Make it evergreen. Make your video timeless, or evergreen, so stay away from holiday themes, specific times of the year, or a certain sale. Once you are in a groove for producing videos, you can jump into videos with specific themes. But for now, focus on a video that will work year-round.

You don't recognize it until you are watching a video that has a leaf blower going on next door, or a trash truck drives by, all obliterating the audio. And the tiny pin-hole mics just don't cut it and are usually too far away from the person's mouth, so investing in a mic you can attach to your camera and then to the person talking, will be clearer to understand and less distracting to the viewer.

Background

Do your best to make sure your background in the video isn't distracting. You don't want to have a mirror on the back wall that shows in the reflection your camera, video light, and the back of you talking to the camera. You also want to make sure you don't have something distracting "poking" out of your head visually.

Length

33% of viewers will stop watching a video after 30 seconds, 45% by one minute, and 60% by two minutes. (AdAge)

Your video should be only as long as it is entertaining. If it can hold your attention for 5 solid minutes then let it run, but generally, 90 seconds to 2 minutes is a great length video, especially one featured on the front of your website.

Once you are done with your video, post it to a video streaming platform like YouTube, Wistia, or Vimeo, and then make sure it is "embedded" into the front page of your website. When you embed a video, it will play right there on your webpage, and not take you to another website to play. We want to keep your viewers on your site and not direct them to other attention-grabbing websites like YouTube.

You can get the embed code once your video is public, by generally going to the "share" button.

The layout is always changing, but you should get a bit of code that looks like this:

```
<iframe width="560" height="315" src="https://www.youtube.com/
embed/ZSpqsGJJilA" title="YouTube video player" frameborder="0"
allow="accelerometer; autoplay; clipboard-write; encrypted-media;
gyroscope; picture-in-picture" allowfullscreen></iframe>
```

Being able to "embed" a video on your site is standard across most platforms and should be as easy as copying and pasting the code into the proper text box to have it appear.

 Pro Tip

1. Make sure to upload your videos directly to the desired platform so they autoplay in the feed.

2. Social Media Platform algorithms favor videos that have been directly uploaded to their platform rather than a link that will take the viewer off of the platform (and away from their ads, which is how Facebook generates revenue.)

3. Also make sure you have them auto captioned on FaceBook. It is something like 85% of videos are muted when viewed on social media. So, people can read what is being said in the video.

4. Plan on posting it every couple of months, in case people missed it the first time in their feed.

Here are a few handy worksheets that you can use to outline and film your next video. You can download them for FREE at BearWade.com/ bookresouces

Content Outline

What problem/pain point is your viewer having that you are hoping to solve?

_____

_____

Why should they listen to you for the solution?

_____

_____

What is your solution?

_____

_____

What should they do if they want your solution? (Call-to-action)

_____

_____

⬇ Download a copy of this worksheet at UnifyYourMarketing.com

Push Record Checklist

☐ Good wardrobe

☐ Good hair & makeup

☐ Good background

☐ Camera on

☐ Camera card formatted

☐ Camera at good height

☐ Camera at good distance

☐ Video lights on

☐ Mic on

☐ Mic level good

☐ Looking at the camera

☐ Take a deep breath

☐ Keep energy up

Push Record

Smile and have fun! You are going to help people!

 Download a copy of this resource at UnifyYourMarketing.com

Gathering Testimonials

How to gather good testimonials

Testimonials are displays of social proof that your company is valuable. Very Valuable. Like gold. It is one thing to say that you are great at what you do, but it is another thing for someone else to say you are great.

Gathering testimonials should be standard practice for you and your company.

What you want in a good testimonial is something short, and states how you solved your happy customer's problem. If you can get a photo of their smiling face, all the better. If you use Google Reviews, great! That will help with your website SEO, so make sure you set up a Google My Business page if you haven't already. Also, adding testimonials to Facebook is great too.

You can even add those testimonials to your website, so you instill more confidence in your viewer's decision to buy from you.

Remember, you can hardly EVER have too many testimonials. Just pile it on! Smother your viewer in overwhelming satisfaction from everyone you've worked with.

If you are struggling to get people to write a testimonial for you, then this is what I do to get it going:

I write it for them, on their behalf, and then let them re-write it or approve it. I thoughtfully write it from their perspective and do my very best to advocate for their image, but at the same time write something that would be helpful for our potential clients to understand.

Another way to get people to write reviews is to offer them an incentive. So give them a discount when they write their review or enter them into a drawing to win something substantial. Make it fun and get as many as you can in the coming year.

Here are a few examples:

"Working on my social media ad was easy and helps my viewers understand what I do clearer."

- April A. -
Midwest Thermography Solutions

"Their ongoing support to publish our work to our community is a godsend."

- Caroline H. -
Crossings

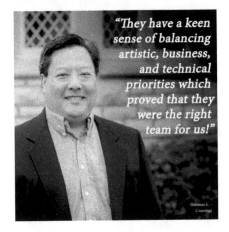

"They have a keen sense of balancing artistic, business, and technical priorities which proved that they were the right team for us!"

- Sherman L. -
Crossings

"Their process was not transactional, it was transformational!"

- Paul D. -
Gateway Swings

I use these four testimonials on my website, print media, social media, hell, I think some other testimonials might be on the back of this book!

CHAPTER 3

KEY TAKEAWAYS

Solidify your brand media

- Curate authentic brand photos
- Create your brand video
- Gather client testimonials

CONGRATULATIONS!

You have now completed Brand Step 1 by defining your brand script, value proposition, and call-to-action.

From there, we worked together to define your logo signature, brand colors, fonts, and additional design elements to create your brand style guide. We've also collected and produced brand photos, brand videos, and testimonials.

Next, you can move on to Brand Step #2 which is all about applying these assets and building your marketing materials.

UNIFY STEP 2

BUILDING

Building your pricing structure, website, social media and print media so your ideal customer can buy from you easily.

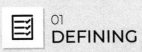
01
DEFINING

02
BUILDING

03
GROWING

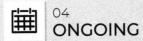
04
ONGOING

05
SCALING

CHAPTER 4

PRICING STRUCTURE

Pricing structure = the solution you provide + the price your customer is willing to pay to solve their problem.

Building is all about building your pricing structure, website, social media and print media so your ideal customer can buy from you easily. Your domain name, website, sales funnel, and social media channels should accurately reflect your business model and pricing structure. The final step in the building phase is to build your print media including brochures, postcards, handouts, and business cards that drive customers into your sales funnel.

What Profitable Businesses Have in Common

The most profitable businesses:

1. Limit their service or product offerings

2. Track and measure their results

3. Produce these results repeatedly

For decades, I didn't do this. Hell, I still struggle with it.

Building a pricing structure that buyers can understand is essential to a profitable business. If viewers don't know what they can buy, or are confused about their options, odds are they won't purchase anything or will need your time and attention to buy from you.

My whole business model was based around someone coming to me with a problem. I would then MacGyver a custom solution for them with the tools and resources that I had. If I didn't have the tools, I went out and bought the new gear and software for that specific job.

I never created a system. And I rarely reused the same specialty gear enough to make back my investment.

So, learn from me and define your business model and the tools (overhead) you need to fulfill those services. This will enable you to build a business that can grow and thrive. This all starts by building your pricing structure. Let's go!

The whole goal of defining your pricing structure is to define the work you will do for the price someone will pay you for it. The more value you bring to your customer, the more you can charge for your product or service. How hard or long you work doesn't actually matter. What they're paying for is you solving their problem with a solution you're proud of and excited to deliver.

People buy products that solve a particular problem at a price they're willing to pay to leave that problem behind.

Hourly vs. fixed price models

Many people charge an hourly rate for their services, but I'm not convinced that hourly models bring repeat business, which is some of the best business to get! It's much easier to sell to an existing customer rather than a "cold lead," someone who you need to build a relationship with before they're ready to purchase.

There is a whole funnel between the top (cold leads) and the bottom (customers) that's why it is so important to define your pricing structure up front. This way you can focus your energy on developing those relationships and be completely transparent about pricing throughout that relationship building.

Also, when you define your pricing structure, you can calculate your fee quicker and take their money sooner. I don't know about you, but I don't want to spend time doing paperwork. I want to make things and help people! So, with a pricing structure, you can get to that sooner.

When you are defining your pricing structure you can also lead the soon-to-be customer through some of the problems they might have and your proven solutions to them.

Productize your offer: real-life example

Like many business owners, I know social media is an amazing business tool, but takes a ton of time. I knew I could pay someone else to do it better, faster, and cheaper. I received over 100 applications for the job after posting it on Indeed, Facebook, and UpWork. Most of the candidates are business owners who specialize in running social media accounts for other companies.

After filtering the applicants, I checked out my top 5 candidate's websites. I looked at the overall look and feel of their website, the quality of their content, learned more about their background and former client work and checked for pricing options. Not a single one had anything about pricing on their website. Despite being ready to pull the trigger on hiring someone, they weren't making it easy to sign on. Alas, I kept going.

I set up interviews for my top 5 candidates. During those interviews, many asked me what I wanted done for my social media accounts or how many posts I wanted weekly. To be honest, I had no clue and I didn't want to mess with it at all, I just wanted to hand it off. I had no desire to keep up with the trends in social media. Instead, I wanted their expertise to guide the number of posts and content in order to build awareness, grow my email database and generate sales.

I had each person put together proposals and most were based on what that person would do with their time, not really the outcome of my investment. I don't need "3 posts a week." I need "track engagements" and "track sales" and "analyze what is working, and scale for growth". See the difference?

This whole process could be a heck of a lot easier if the candidates had clearly outlined their pricing structure on their website. I wouldn't have to waste time with interviews if I knew exactly what they were offering and the price they were willing to do it for.

Use your pricing structure to guide your customer through a journey of success.

This might seem a little wonky, but hear me out on this. By using your experience as an expert in your industry, you can craft the way a newbie can be set up for success by purchasing from you, in a particular order. For instance, let's take Subway restaurants, in the way you order. You walk in the door, someone greets you from behind the counter. There is a sign at one end of the counter that says "Order Here." There you are met with a person who will handmake your sandwich for you either custom or from one of the menu pre-designed options.

First you start with the type of bread, the size of sandwich, protein selection, cheese, toppings, condiments and then they wrap it up for you with a napkin, because they know that sometimes sandwiches can be messy.

They ask you if you would like a dessert or drink with your order, because they know that you'll be thirsty and might want a little sweet finish after your sandwich. It all comes in a narrow clear plastic bag with a big handle, easy to carry to your table or car, while navigating the drink station.

Pro Tip

If you are afraid to post your prices online, do the work to better understand and communicate your value proposition. This highlights how your customers get a good return on their investments and saves you the headache of weeding out clients unwilling to pay the price for your skill.

See? They have used their experience with eating and selling millions of these sandwiches to streamline your process of having a successful meal.

How can you do this in your business? What is common knowledge to you that someone who is just starting out in your industry need?

Shape the buyer experience around that process. You get the up-sell cash, and they are set up for success! A win-win!

Focus on benefits and not just features

Clients don't care what you do. They care about the results of what you do. Social media managers DO need to define how many posts, who is creating the content ideas, who is responsible for posting content and who is monitoring the comments, but more importantly, all of that work should be focused 100% on the goal of why we are doing it: to get more sales or to get more leads.

To build awareness, grow my email database, and grow my sales

It would be far easier to approach this process by searching for a social media manager who advertises that they can accomplish these things. It's even better if my potential solutions providers share packages with a tiered pricing structure.

Focusing on YOU: Building Your Pricing Structure

Grab a pen and paper. If you're into spreadsheets, this would be an excellent time to sketch one out or even open your computer.

Start by figuring out what it takes behind the scenes to get one specific job completed.

In-House Pricing Guide

1. In the first column, put a service you offer. For now, just one service. Keep it specific.

2. In the next column, List all of the tasks that need to be done to provide that service.

3. In a third column, list all of the tools, resources, and people it takes to provide that service.

4. Now, start to ballpark what you think this service would cost each time you did it. Of course, you are going to have big tools you use for many projects. Factor a fraction of that cost into each individual service.

5. Research what other people in your field offer and charge by searching on the internet and asking colleagues. If you are way under your peers, add more value; if you are way over, figure out how to streamline your process, or justify your reasoning for that higher ticket cost.

6. Go back to Step 1 of this process to flush out the behind the scenes cost of each service you offer.

Customer Tiers and Packages

Once you have figured out your behind the scenes cost for each service, you can transition over to packaging the customer deliverables.

1. Using your most requested service, create the first tier of your pricing structure.

2. Next, define for your customer what they will receive upon purchasing that tier or package. Remember, *focus on benefits and not just features.*

EXERCISE   YOUR PRICING STRUCTURE

3. Create a price that is easy to understand, logical and transparent. This empowers the customer to make an informed decision. You will do more harm than good in advertising a lower price and surprising the customer with additional costs before final checkout.

4. Create one or two additional tiers adding on services, keeping in mind the behind-the-scenes cost while conveying the benefits to your customer.

5. Create a graphic to feature prominently on your website, print materials, etc with your pricing tiers. Be sure it clearly shows the features, the problems they solve, the cost and how to purchase. Make it quick and easy for the customer to buy.

6. Test your tiers for a few months to determine if they are performing well or if you need to analyze and restructure to better fit your customers needs.

 Download a copy of this worksheet at UnifyYourMarketing.com

 Pro Tip

Don't over complicate it. Most great businesses have 3 "packages" they offer. Think through what you want to offer at a very basic level, and add one or two services on top to create higher tier packages.

Your pricing structure should be easy to understand for both you and your viewers. Those packages guide your prospects into electing the best choice for themselves. If you are a social media manager, your three tiers should show us how many posts, reels, stories, videos, memes, etc you would be posting to get the desired result we are looking for. Then offer the cost of that investment and a "Buy Now" button next to it, that lets us buy from you without needing your attention.

Most of all, your pricing structure will determine how you will spend your days. Your most basic package should be a thing you love doing.

Defining your pricing structure is all about how your business is going to end up running. No matter your type of business, your pricing structure defines how you will spend your time and what you will have to fulfill.

BASIC

✓ 1 post to reels/week
✓ 2 posts to feed/week
✓ 3 posts to stories/week

$49
per month

SELECT THIS PLAN

PRO

POPULAR

✓ 2 posts to reels/week
✓ 4 posts to feed/week
✓ 6 posts to stories/week
+ Weekly analytics report

$299
per month

SELECT THIS PLAN

ENTERPRISE

✓ 3 posts to reels/week
✓ 6 posts to feed/week
✓ 10 posts to stories/week
+ Weekly analytics report
+ Custom growth strategies

$1999
per month

SELECT THIS PLAN

Having clear pricing options with listed benefits can enable your customers to make informed decisions.

 Pro Tip

Set up your online payment buttons to automatically populate customer information, like stored debit/credit card info, name, address, and email. If I have to go find my wallet to buy your service, the added friction may stop me from pulling the trigger and you might lose out!

CHAPTER 4

KEY TAKEAWAYS

Define your pricing structure

- Identify the problem you're solving
- Solidify your offer and how it solves the problem
- Use the problem and your solution to determine your services and pricing structure

CHAPTER 5

BUILDING YOUR WEBSITE

Convey the look and feel of your business through a clear and concise website.

 CONSIDER HIRING A CONTRACTOR

Why Websites Are King in A Social Media World

57% of internet users say they won't recommend a business with a poorly designed website on mobile.

Websites are still very valuable even with the prevalence and influence of social media platforms. Why? Because YOU own them. You get to house and control all of your content the way you want, and 100% of your viewers have access to it.

Your social media posts only reach 4% of your followers' feed during their scroll. 4%!!! If your posts gain traction with followers and friends interacting with your content, then the algorithms trigger more placements to more followers.

But social media algorithms change rapidly, and it is difficult to maintain complete control over your content. This is why having a good website is vital.

Websites can come in various shapes and sizes and have become rich with content. Some sites are one page long scrolling sites to mimic social media feeds, others are hubs that direct you to main pillars of content, some have subpages and even non-accessible pages.

The best website is the one that wows your visitors with who you are and converts them into paying customers and can be found easily. Your website needs to be specific to your business and to the way YOUR ideal customer likes to receive their information.

Rely on the foundational work you did at the beginning of this book. To remind yourself what is most important to your ideal customer. Build your website around them.

Your website should tell your customers:

- The challenge you solve for
- What services or products they can buy from you (and the result of making that commitment)
- How they purchase it (pricing structure??)
- The type of customer support they can expect (how it feels to do business with you)

If you're struggling to be able to capture and communicate all these pieces, you haven't figured out your business model yet. You need to go back to Step 1. Your website is a big mirror to reflect back to you what your business is about and where there may be holes in your identity.

You only have about 10–20 seconds to convince your visitors to stay on your site. Make sure your website is engaging enough to keep them on the page and increase your return on investment for building your website in the first place.

But first! Let's chat about the 3 different kinds of websites.

Three Types of Websites

In general, there are three different kinds of "websites":

- The Digital Brochure
- The Online Store
- The Publication Hub

It's quite possible that your website has elements of all three, depending on your business. Let's unpack the three levels of good websites.

The digital brochure

A digital brochure website shows off the services or products you offer, and adds a ton of validity to your brand online. It might not be the first entry point to your brand, but should help you close the sale. If you are just getting a website up and running for your business, start with a solid digital brochure.

Examples of a digital brochure:

National Museum of Natural History (naturalhistory.si.edu)

American Red Cross (redcross.org)

The general public will judge you, your business, and value-based upon how well your site looks put together, speaks to their needs and is easy to engage in your services.

Businesses that benefit: small business, restaurant owner, lawn mowing business, a plumber, or consultant, or coach, any service-oriented business.

The online store

The online store gives the customer the option to buy directly from the site. I love the idea of sitting on the proverbial beach and making passive income by helping people purchase a solution that we've already developed.

For me, the ultimate goal in business is to have people buying from our company without me having to directly sell it! Creating an online store is a major step towards achieving that goal. If people have to go through YOU (or any human) to purchase, you have created a major bottleneck in the potential growth of your business.

Examples of an online store:

Target (target.com)

Amazon (amazon.com)

Can you imagine if Jeff Bezos, the founder of Amazon.com still took every customer order? What a s#!t show that would be! Okay, I'm not saying that you are going to be generating billions of dollars per year with your store, but if you don't productize your offering and offer it for sale online, then what chance do you have?!

This is why every website should sell something directly through its interface. In 2020 alone, e-commerce more than doubled in the U.S. More and more people are shopping online.

Positioning your company to be where the people are, with less friction to exchange your solutions for their money, is necessary for business growth.

The publication hub

Finally, the last major "type" or characteristic of a successful website is being a publication hub. This is vital because one major tool to bring visitors to your website is to create valuable and engaging content.

If you consistently post new content, you will quickly have a robust website with lots of content on it that can be searched and indexed by search engines like Google and Bing.

Examples of a publication hub:

Buzzfeed (buzzfeed.com)

NPR (npr.org)

This is what marketing experts refer to as SEO, or search engine optimization. SEO is a fancy way for a search engine like Google to rank how helpful your website will be when a user types in different search terms. When your website is home to a wealth of high-quality content that is relevant to your brand and product offerings, you will have better content for Google and other search engines to rank your site.

There are plenty of additional strategies and tools you can use to rank higher in search results. Work with a SEO specialist to bring your content to the people who need it.

We will talk more about creating a content strategy and schedule in Brand Step 4. For now, know that creating additional content for your website will help further the value it provides as a digital brochure.

Creating a Mockup of Your Website

As a visual person who likes to get my hands on things (ahem, video producer) this is just a practical way to do it rather than outlining my business plan on paper. But before you dive into actually designing your website, create a wireframe or website mockup.

You can have a lot of fun playing around with your mockup before building it out as a functioning website. This way you are focused on the meat of your website, and not the details of coding and customizing.

Unify Your Marketing Website

You will probably recognize this site when you visit UnifyYourMarketing.com for awesome resources and downloads.

You can also see that the brand standards for this site are consistent with everything in this book! This is an example of using brand colors, fonts, and imagery to tie the brand together. There is no doubt that this site belongs with this book based on their shared brand standards.

Creating a Site Map

Another option is to write an outline of your site map. Include all of the pages you want to have on your site. Then arrange the hierarchy and flow of your ideal customer journey to experience your website.

I like to start drawing boxes and lines, like the example here, but you can also just create a traditional outline starting with the homepage. Then the next layer are the pages you can get to through the navigation both at the top and bottom of your website as well as any other entry points from the front page to additional pages or posts. Then from there you can include additional layers but mapping this out on paper can really help you or your website developer catch the vision of what you are expecting to build.

So, what should your website site map look like? If you currently have one, how would you change it?.

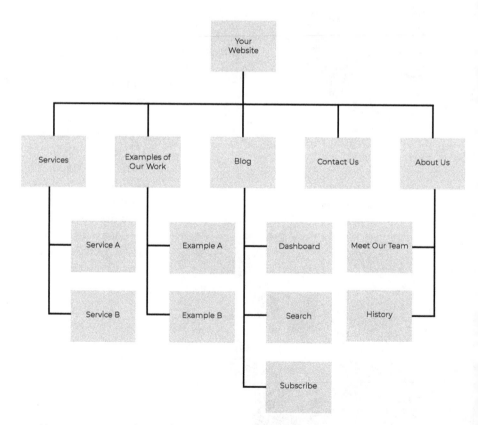

Here you can see that we've mapped out a website that has a landing page, with five tabs on it, and then secondary information behind, or below, that.

Creating a Site Map

Start with this outline below, grab a pencil and fill in the pages of your website. Start with a homepage, then define the most important layers of information that your clients will come to your website looking for.

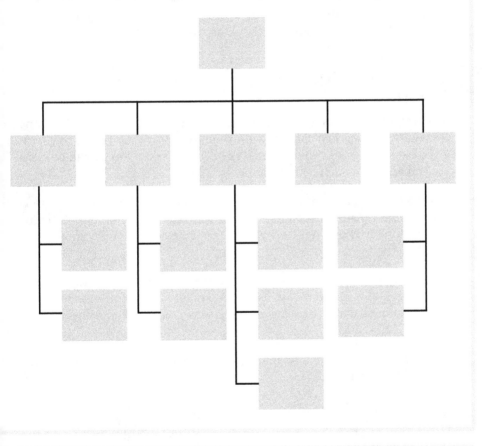

Ten Elements Your Website NEEDS to Close Deals and Make You Money

There are 10 valuable elements your website needs right now to look more professional and convert visitors into customers.

1. Top menu

Place a clear logo in the upper left corner of your navigation bar with basic navigational buttons. Also include a primary call-to-action button in the upper right corner of your website in the navigation bar.

It has been researched and reported by HotJar.com that the upper right corner of your navigation bar is highly clicked over other locations when placing your CTA.

And as far buttons, in the main navigation bar, keep it to 3-5 total buttons. Too many options can contend with where you want the viewer to go and paralyze them or lead them astray. The buttons at the top should be clear, set you apart, and drive conversions.

For example: For a dentist's office, you would see a logo, hero photo of "white coat caring for a patient" and a way to schedule an appointment. If they don't find that right away, they may quickly move onto another site that is better organized.

Don't worry about fitting everything you want to include into the main navigation. The additional items can be added to the footer menu. Think instead about what your customer needs to be able to find within 5 seconds.

You want to make sure that the mobile navigation "hamburger" menu (box with 3 horizontal lines) is formatted correctly too, and is easy to click with a push of a finger.

2. Hero shot

A Hero shot is the one photograph or background video that highlights your product or service and your happy customers. You want this photo or slow-motion video to be as clear and vibrant as possible because it "speaks 1,000 words" in a short-attention-span world, and can communicate ideas faster than reading words or watching a video.

Hiring a professional to minimize variable and emphasis features is recommended. This one photo can make or break your viewer's experience.

If the photograph is good, it goes a long way to your viewer's perception of what they think of your company.

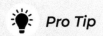

Pro Tip

Using silent video or moving gif in the background for your hero shot can bring movement and a richer understanding of the concept you are hoping to portray.

3. Headline/subheadline

Your headline should be one of the major key elements in the hierarchy of content communication. Your headline should NOT be cute, or vague, or ambiguous. It should state what you do, the problem you solve, or the people you serve.

According to an article on the website DigitalDoughnut.com, on average, 8 out of 10 people will read headline copy, but only 2 out of 10 will read the rest.

This headline should be the result of your brand script which is Step 1 of the Brand Steps. If you skipped that part go back now!! Remember, your foundation will hold up the rest of your business.

In 3 seconds a new viewer should be able to understand what you do or who you serve just from the hero photo and headline. If it takes more than 3 seconds, refine, hone, and test on a variety of people until it is simplified enough.

Businesses who are location-based should also include their address or city in the headline.

When a new user can tell you what you do accurately after only a few seconds of being on your website, you'll know you've honed it well.

Having a subheadline is helpful to add empathy to your headline or hit home why they should choose you. This font should be smaller, the same color, and below the headline.

Here are some examples:

We Are Denver's Plumbing Experts
See why we have been rated 5 stars on Google three years in a row!

Nacho' Ordinary Mexican Food
See our zesty yet refreshing Yelp reviews and why people keep coming back for more!

Wichita's #1 Realtor®
Find your forever dream home at the right price today

We Help Leaders Define Their Future
Planners designed for executives, managers, and creators

4. Call-to-action

47% of websites have a clear call-to-action button that takes users 3 seconds or less to see.

The CTA, as defined in Brand Step #1, as part of your brand script needs to be highlighted over and over on your landing page. Place it on the navigation bar, below your subheadline on your hero shot, and down the page a handful of other times.

Making CTAs look like buttons created a 45% boost in clicks for CreateDebate.

Emails with a single call-to-action increased clicks 371% and sales 1617%. (WordStream)

Adding CTAs to your Facebook page can increase the click-through rate by 285%. (AdRoll)

Sometimes the CTA is "Book a Discovery Call" or "Buy Now" or "Take our Assessment." The CTA is really up to you but should be in a bold highlight color that is easy to find with a quick scroll of the page.

5. Flow

When we think about the hierarchy of content on your landing page, we want to make sure we have a broad overview near the top and more rich details near the bottom. Don't get the viewer stuck in the weeds and confused too early.

Start broad and then the farther they go into your site the more you can serve them your knowledge and understanding of their issues you are hoping to help them with.

Before working on your site, consider a first-time viewer of your site. Jot down your flow of information, and then make sure that it makes sense to a first time visitor. Keep your language easy to read and accessible to sixth-grader reading level.

Use your words sparingly and use them deliberately. Most websites have too many words and congest the flow of information for a website. There isn't a word count that I recommend for your front page. Just be mindful of the ratio between images, illustrations, videos, white space, and words.

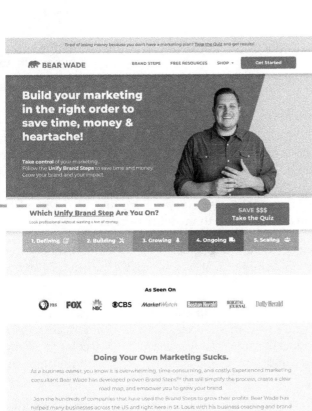

Tired of losing money because you don't have a marketing plan? Take the Quiz and get results!

🐻 BEAR WADE   BRAND STEPS   FREE RESOURCES   SHOP ▾   Get Started

Build your marketing in the right order to save time, money & heartache!

Take control of your marketing.
Follow the **Unify Brand Steps** to save time and money.
Grow your brand and your impact.

Which Unify Brand Step Are You On?
Look professional without wasting a ton of money.

SAVE $$$
Take the Quiz

1. Defining ✏️   2. Building 🔨   3. Growing 📊   4. Ongoing 💬   5. Scaling 🎯

As Seen On

🅿️ PBS   **FOX**   🦚 NBC   **●CBS**   *MarketWatch*   Boston Herald   BERGITAL JOURNAL   Daily Herald

Doing Your Own Marketing Sucks.

As a business owner, you know it is overwhelming, time-consuming, and costly. Experienced marketing consultant Bear Wade has developed proven Brand Steps™ that will simplify the process, create a clear road map, and empower you to grow your brand.

Join the hundreds of companies that have used the Brand Steps to grow their profits. Bear Wade has helped many businesses across the US and right here in St. Louis with his business coaching and brand development strategies. If you're interested in working with one of the leading St. Louis marketing consultants, contact Bear Wade or explore our site for more information.

Save Money On Your Marketing

FREE Resources
FREE

Unify Secrets
How to Double Your Income
Invest in the Best Course
Unify Launch Sequence
Top 5 Places To Use Video
Push Record Checklist
A Better Website Checklist

DIY Solutions
🛠️

Unify Brand Steps
Unify Content Pipeline
Unify Marketing Audit
Unify Brand Script
Unify Content Guide

Done-For-You Solutions
☕

Quick Win Video
Unify Brand Kit
Unify Launch
Unify Website
Unify Stage
Unify My Videos
Unify Reach

UNIFY MY   **UNIFY+**

Don't use insider language and nomenclature or acronyms that are code to the viewer. Don't make them work any harder than they have to to understand what you are trying to say.

6. Additional images

In addition to your hero, choose a handful of additional images to supplement and balance your narrative information on the site. Be sure to reference your brand photos defined in step one to ensure all photos are cohesive in look and feel. Use photos of your target demographic here, happy customers, or additional images of your product or service. Like your words, keep them clear, and use them deliberately.

When choosing your additional images, consider dynamic diversity. Yes, that includes race, age, and gender. It also includes diversity in the way you tell a story.

Capture wide shots, mid shots, close up and ultra close-ups. Or highlight specific features or details of your product. Show life without this, using this, and after this product or service. Consider pattern and color in picking your additional images and how to incorporate them into the flow and design of your site.

Analyze big company websites, like Apple and Microsoft. See how they feature their products using photography and additional images.

7. Lead magnets

A lead magnet is a free piece of highly valuable content in exchange for someone's email address. Whether it be a PDF, webinar, coupon, or exclusive video, this lead magnet is designed to provide incredible value to your visitors. It should also provide continuous value and buying opportunities from you via email all while securing leads by continuing to be published on your website or a landing page in perpetuity.

This is a test drive to your brand. Will they like, know, and trust you after having access to your lead magnet? If not, it isn't valuable enough. If so, you can create a tribe that will certainly buy from you down the road, as you continue to deliver value to them over time.

Your lead magnet should be "advertised" or featured prominently on your landing page with a place for them to type in their email address. Have a graphic of the "cover" of your freebie and place it next to a short description and email address fill-in form.

Doing Your Own Marketing Sucks.

As a business owner, you know it is overwhelming, time-consuming, and costly. Experienced marketing consultant Bear Wade has developed proven Brand Steps™ that will simplify the process, create a clear road map, and empower you to grow your brand.

Join the hundreds of companies that have used the Brand Steps to grow their profits. Bear Wade has helped many businesses across the US and right here in St. Louis with his business coaching and brand development strategies. If you're interested in working with one of the leading St. Louis marketing consultants, contact Bear Wade or explore our site for more information.

Save Money On Your Marketing

FREE Resources
FREE

Unify Secrets
How to Double Your Income
Invest in the Best Course
Unify Launch Sequence
Top 5 Places To Use Video
Push Record Checklist
A Better Website Checklist

DIY Solutions

Unify Brand Steps
Unify Content Pipeline
Unify Marketing Audit
Unify Brand Script
Unify Content Guide

Done-For-You Solutions

Quick Win Video
Unify Brand Kit
Unify Launch
Unify Website
Unify Stage
Unify My Videos
Unify Reach

UNIFY MY MARKETING SHOW
with BEAR WADE

GET MARKETING GUIDANCE
SUBMIT YOUR QUESTIONS

UNIFY+

GROW YOUR EMPIRE.

Monthly members get exclusive access to all Unify offerings.

Get Membership

Become a Certified Unify Instructor
Find a meaningful way to help others grow their business

Enroll Today!

UNIFY CLIENT WINS!

Share your big wins on Instagram @TheBearWade

This form should be connected to your CRM, which we will get to in Brand Step 3, and automatically send a private link to your freebie after they fill out your form.

Your customers expect value, so make sure your button says "download now" or "gain access" or "view now" rather than "submit", "subscribe" or "sign-up" something more active and less passive. Also, make sure this button is a vibrant color so it catches their attention.

Having a strong lead magnet, or many lead magnets, is that it collects email addresses of your prospects. You can add them to your email list and continue to reach out to them with high-value content eventually turning them into a paying customer.

An email database is yours. You own it and it is specific to your company. This list of people have reached out to you in one way or another and found value in what your brand brings to their possible issues. This is something that is way more valuable than social media followers, where you don't own them. If the algorithm changes, you have lost contact with them. You might have noticed this over the past few years with Facebook.

Only a small percentage of people that follow your business page actually see your posts in their feed. And if you boost a post, which costs money, your reach goes up exponentially, but it is a pay-to-play model, where sending emails can be much more effective and economical.

If you are getting traffic to your site, but not many people are requesting access to your lead magnet, there are a number of changes you can make. You could:

- Change the "submit" button color, or
- Swap out a new graphic, or
- Experiment with the location within the flow of your content.

Pro Tip

Adjusting the cover photo size and placing the CTA button right below the headline can generate a 47% increase in click-through rate. Making CTAs look like buttons and personalized CTAs convert much higher rates of visitors to paid customers.

Test different elements until your signup rate goes up. Ensure you pair any changes with the promotion of your site or product to get adequate visitors to test the success of any changes.

Next steps: make it crystal clear

Next, on your landing page should be a simple process that clearly defines the next steps in working with you.

As Donald Miller of Storybrand says, "If you confuse, you lose."

If people don't know the next steps, there is a much higher chance that they won't take them. So, spelling it out, which might seem obvious to you, can help guide your viewer into becoming a paying customer.

Here are a few examples of a simple process:

Apply Online > Get Approved > Buy Your Dream Home

Book a Discovery Call > Receive a Proposal > We Build Your Website

Book appointment > We Fix your Dishwasher > You can reclaim your kitchen

Shop Now > Buy Custom Computer > Experience new games like never before

8. List your ideal customers (so people know you're talking to THEM)

List out your ideal customers. Name them here. Let your viewer's know that this is for them, or that you aren't the right fit for them. Doing this can really funnel the right people to you, and save you (and them) heartache in the long run.

Tell your viewers who you serve is the first step in quality service! So spell it out. Define your different target or ideal customers and state it in this section.

There is a saying, "If you aim at nothing, you'll hit it every time." Spell out your target you are hoping to hit, so to speak.

Some examples of audiences:

Small business owners, pickup truck owners, first-time homeowners, kids 4-6th grade, dog owners, kindle owners, etc.

9. Trust builders: show the social proof

Solidify visitors' trust by including social proof and testimonials. Using customer testimonials, customer logos, and case studies can all help tighten the bond between them and your brand.

Social proof is about taking your company's social circle and letting them speak for you, about you, to people like them. Adding this credibility to your brand is so valuable to growing trust with your potential customers.

According to Spiegel Research Center, about 95% of customers read reviews before making a purchase so get your fans to create noise for you!

It is one thing to say you are Tulsa's #1 Honda Dealer, but it takes a mom with three kids that loves the reliability and safety of her Odyssey minivan. This shows people just like her why they will love their new car too!

You can NOT have too many testimonials. You don't have to post them all at the same time. You can rotate them around between your eblasts, social media and website.

How would you feel if you scrolled down the page of the dealer's Odyssey landing page and there were literally 500 positive reviews of this van? It

Doing Your Own Marketing Sucks.

As a business owner, you know it is overwhelming, time-consuming, and costly. Experienced marketing consultant Bear Wade has developed proven Brand Steps™ that will simplify the process, create a clear road map, and empower you to grow your brand.

Join the hundreds of companies that have used the Brand Steps to grow their profits. Bear Wade has helped many businesses across the US and right here in St. Louis with his business coaching and brand development strategies. If you're interested in working with one of the leading St. Louis marketing consultants, contact Bear Wade or explore our site for more information.

Save Money On Your Marketing

FREE Resources	DIY Solutions	Done-For-You Solutions
Unify Secrets	Unify Brand Steps	Quick Win Video
How to Double Your Income	Unify Content Pipeline	Unify Brand Kit
Invest in the Best Course	Unify Marketing Audit	Unify Launch
Unify Launch Sequence	Unify Brand Script	Unify Website
Top 5 Places To Use Video	Unify Content Guide	Unify Stage
Push Record Checklist		Unify My Videos
A Better Website Checklist		Unify Reach

UNIFY MY MARKETING SHOW

with BEAR WADE

GET MARKETING GUIDANCE

SUBMIT YOUR QUESTIONS

UNIFY+

GROW YOUR EMPIRE.

Monthly members get exclusive access to all Unify offerings.

Get Membership

Become a Certified Unify Instructor
Find a meaningful way to help others grow their business

Enroll Today!

UNIFY CLIENT WINS!

Share your big wins on Instagram @TheBearWade

kind of sells itself at this point. If you can get a photo of that person smiling, even better! It adds validity to your case, and having 500 smiles staring back at you instills that "I can be one of these people easily too."

The Edelman Trust Barometer reports that over 60% of the 32,000 people surveyed trusted experts and peers over other sources, which tells us that getting our happy customers to talk to their friends, family, and colleagues about us is going to bring the warmest leads.

10. Footer

The footer of your landing page should be the same on every page of your website, unless there is a good reason for customizing it so your viewer can get comfortable with getting around your site easily. Keep it tidy, but the amount of information here can be extensive to help people access more in-depth content they might be seeking.

Include navigation links to:

- Company and staff information
- Legal notices
- Social media links
- Your contact information
- Media and press links (like your logo and brand kits)
- Other miscellaneous information

FREE Resources

- Unify Secrets
- How to Double Your Income
- Invest in the Best Course
- Unify Launch Sequence
- Top 5 Places To Use Video
- Push Record Checklist
- A Better Website Checklist

DIY Solutions

- Unify Brand Steps
- Unify Content Pipeline
- Unify Marketing Audit
- Unify Brand Script
- Unify Content Guide

Done-For-You Solutions

- Quick Win Video
- Unify Brand Kit
- Unify Launch
- Unify Website
- Unify Stage
- Unify My Videos
- Unify Reach

UNIFY MY MARKETING
SHOW
with BEAR WADE

GET MARKETING GUIDANCE

SUBMIT YOUR QUESTIONS

UNIFY+

GROW YOUR EMPIRE.

Monthly members get exclusive access to all Unify offerings.

Get Membership

Become a Certified Unify Instructor

Find a meaningful way to help others grow their business.

UNIFY CERTIFIED

Enroll Today!

UNIFY CLIENT WINS!

Share your big wins on Instagram @TheBearWade

WORK THE UNIFY BRAND STEPS FASTER | Get marketing advice you can easily apply to your business.

Who is Bear Wade?

Unify Creative Agency

Treadwell Data

Here is an example of a website mockup we did for Treadwell Data, a software consulting company that works with non-profit organizations to keep track of their fundraising initiatives and reporting data.

You can notice the ten elements of website design present here.

1. Top menu

2. Hero shot

3. Headline/ subheadline

4. Call-to-action

5. Flow

Notice the hierarchy outlined in this design, and the move from general to specific information.

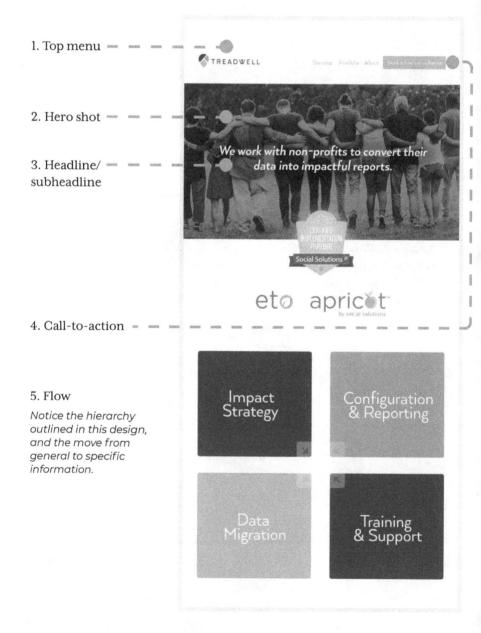

Data drives your organization. It is how you measure the people reached, lives changed. It is how you decide where and how your funds are invested. Refined data can give an accurate assessment of your organization's goals and success.

So what happens when community impact is not easy to quantify? When your numbers aren't making the impression they should? When reporting and grant writing becomes more difficult? What do you need to make your data work for you?

What you need is someone to translate your data into discernible stories of success; dollars into services, donations into hope and grants into thriving communities.

This is what Treadwell does. We make your data work for you when every dollar is a precious commodity and transparency is paramount. We do this by driving nonprofit performance through our programs and processes. We create personal systems designed for your organization and train your team on how to keep your data working so you can keep helping.

6. Additional images

Book a Free Consultation

7. Lead magnet
(In this case another call-to-action)

8. List your ideal customer

"The Treadwell team is very thoughtful in their approach toward design and has a very thorough discovery process.

We have a greater understanding of how ETO can help inform the work we do every day."

– Barb Hadley –
VP of Education and Workforce Development at Project Home

9. Trust builders

Insider knowledge, outsider perspective

HOME
BOOK A CONSULTATION
OUR SERVICES
RESOURCES
OUR PORTFOLIO
WORK WITH US
ABOUT US

Book a Free Consultation

Contact Us

10. Footer

https://bearwade.com/

https://bearwade.com/

The top is the overall grade given by Google Page Speed Insights and after having the work done to optimize images, javascript, lazy loading, among other nerdy shit, you can see that it now loads much faster!

Page Speed

39% of people will stop engaging with a website if images won't load or take too long to load.

Google: "Page Speed Insights" and go to the website from Google. There you can put in your website address and get a report back on how fast or slow your site is on both desktop and mobile.

Finding a person skilled in this particular trade of optimizing site speed is valuable to the ranking on Google and will likely lower your bounce rate, which is how many people "bounce" off your site right away, because of factors such as slow loading times.

You can find freelancers on platforms like Upwork or Fivver. Look for freelancers who offer packages so you can streamline your search and get to work faster. You'll give them full access to your website and website hosting server to do so. And this should be a one-and-done service unless you go through a major site redesign, then you might want to have it re-optimized again.

Page Layout

38% of people will stop engaging with a website if the content or layout is unattractive.

You need to make sure your website is responsive, which means that the design, layout, and flow of content translates between desktop, laptop, tablet, and mobile browsing devices.

In the web design world there is a way of designing called User Experience (UX) and it is all about how a new user interacts with your website (or app). They think about flow of information, accessibility to all abilities, font sizes, contrast, and overall aesthetics of the site as well as the overall functionality.

They also consider how a website translates between desktop and mobile devices and creates a seamless experience between the two so no matter what the user or what their device, you have the same experience.

Make sure you check all of these different browsing options and optimize the settings (and sometimes code) to get the best results.

If you don't know this by now, websites are a never-ending ongoing process. You can always make them better as you go along, and add more value to your reader. Keep evolving it and making it the best experience for your viewers. You have to celebrate your new site, even if it isn't "perfect" but it is launched! It is WAY better than anything you have ever had before, and it is a great platform to work from. Hooray!

CHAPTER 5

KEY TAKEAWAYS

Build your company website

- Learn about the types of websites
- Be sure your website has the 10 elements every website needs
  1. Top menu
  2. Hero shot
  3. Headline/subheadline
  4. Call-to-action
  5. Flow
  6. Additional images
  7. Lead magnets
  8. Ideal customer profiles
  9. Trust builders
  10. Footer

CHAPTER 6

UNIFY YOUR MEDIA

Visually align your digital and print media for consistency and clarity.

CONSIDER HIRING A CONTRACTOR

Social Media

We've all heard that the average person needs to see and hear your brand more than seven times before they will interact with it which in marketing is referred to as the Rule of 7.

However, more research has come out and could be up to 24 times a person needs to see your brand before they will act. For that reason, keep running that brand script. Remind people that you understand their problem and that you have a solution they can trust and that has worked for you.

Social Media is a sticky wicket these days. It is undeniably popular. It is a source for entertainment, keeping tabs on your friends, sharing your life updates, disseminating information, and there is no denying that it is sometimes popular for the wrong reasons.

From the endorphin-inducing design, never-ending scroll, and elusive algorithms, it is hard to win with growing your business through social media. But there is a place for it, especially if you have money to advertise on it. Social media has always been a pay-to-play arena— either in money, time, or attention.

[Now, don't get me wrong, social media CAN be an amazing tool for growth, knowledge, and positive social change.]

No one social media platform is perfect. And trying to post to all of them, in the most optimized way for that specific algorithm's needs, is expensive and draining.

We have found that followers from one platform won't jump to another platform, so you have to build your follower base on each channel separately.

Set up a few social media accounts on the platforms and stake a claim there. Secure EVERY platform with the same username— even the ones you won't be using. Your social media handles should match across channels so your customers can easily find you on each platform.

Linking your social media channels back to your website and your website to your social media channels can help build your search engine ranking and create other opportunities for others to find you on platforms they are already on.

Update your profile images

For each cover photo and profile photo, use the same images you have for your website. Use the same hero image for your cover photo, and your icon/emblem for your profile photo. Keep it unified over all of your different channels, so it is easy to identify your brand no matter what platform they are on.

You will learn how to nuance your messaging depending on platforms because each audience engages differently. For now, keep all of the messaging all matching.

Don't forget to let your existing network and customers know to follow you on these channels, and interact with you!

Social media pillars of content

We have found it is ideal to define different "pillars" or topics for your social media posts. For Red Meat Lover, we defined nine major pillars or topics that we wanted to wrap our content around for social media.

1. Meat America (our travel cooking show)
2. Recipe from our library
3. Biteseez (a short video of a bite-sized cooking hack)
4. Podcast (clip or sound bite from the podcast)
5. Meat the team (feature one of the team members)
6. Brand highlight/giveaway
7. Feature a fan's cook / success / testimonial / YouTube comment
8. Quote or meme
9. New recipe video release

Here are our top 9 focuses for the Bear Wade brand content schedule. You'll see it is a balance of promo, free resources, community engagement, community highlighting, and new content.

1. Brand step feature
2. Client testimonials/feature
3. New show episode
4. Marketing tip or trick
5. Engagement poll/survey/"show me your…"

6. Challenges and giveaways

7. Submit your questions

8. Free resources

9. Product offering

Defining this not only guides content publishers but content creators and everyone is on the same page. And while you are planning out upcoming content you might see where you have holes in your content like you still need to pick a new team member to feature this month, or you might hear a funny quote in the hallway that could be used as a meme. Or you might have a conversation with a customer on the phone which turns into a testimonial.

"Jab jab jab, right hook"

Gary Vaynerchuk, or, Gary Vee as he is known to his more than 1 million Twitter followers is a thought leader on marketing and content creation. He suggests balancing out our content which he calls, "jab jab jab, right hook" meaning you should offer value, offer value, offer value then ask for the sale. If you are always asking, you will fatigue your audience.

The point here is to strategically balance how your audience receives messaging from you.

Although I don't really like the analogy of "fighting" with your customer, I do get what he is saying. Find that golden ratio of value offering to sales.

Going off of Gary Vee's philosophy, it seems like 3:1. I think you can never make that first number too high. Give, give, give. Serve before you sell.

Print Media: It's Not Just For The Geriatric

With all the work you've put in so far, print media will be a cake-walk. It's about creating the in-person shareables that have your brand script, brand identity and photography incorporated into either a brochure, post card, poster, flyer, handout, menu, etc., and formatting it to your desired needs.

Creating a one-sheet

When creating your print media be sure to create a handout, often called a one-sheet as a handy, low-cost tool to hand out to prospective customers. This one-page handout, printed in color, is perfect for meetings, conferences, etc and provides a quick and easily digestible summary of

Pro Tip

Use the design of your website as inspiration! There is no reason to design your one-sheet to look any different than your website. We want it to look unified, so don't over think this step. You've already created all of the elements, you just need to format them for print.

your business. Include details such as your logo, brand colors, hero image, brand script, website, social media handles, call-to-action, and contact information. It can be just one side or double sided front and back and will provide immense value to you in your sales process.

This is also a great way to test your info and address any FAQs you might be getting over and over. You don't have to print 1000 brochures right away. Print a few to start and adjust over time as your needs change. The key is to test your one-sheet and see if it connects with your audience and converts viewers into sales. If your customers are still confused about what you do or the service you offer, make adjustments!

Treadwell Data

Again, working with Treadwell Data, we designed their trade show handouts to look and feel like their website using the same brand elements. Notice the similarities between their website and their print handout?

Print Handouts

Website

CHAPTER 6

KEY TAKEAWAYS

Update your social media with your new brand identity

- Update all profile images
- Determine your pillars of content
- Update your print media

HOLY COW!

Look how much you've accomplished! Be proud of yourself and the work you've put in. Now that you've solidified your pricing structure, have a website built or refreshed, created your social media platforms that reflects your new identity as well as producing at least one piece of sharable printed media, it is time to start growing this thing!

You've done a TON of hard work! Be sure to celebrate it and then, put batteries in the ol' megaphone and start to spread this message to the world! You are ready for primetime. You and your brand are badasses. Fist pump. Let's do this!

UNIFY STEP 3

GROWING

Use customer relationship management software to nurture your current clientele, reach new audiences and grow sales.

01
DEFINING

02
BUILDING

03
GROWING

04
ONGOING

05
SCALING

Congratulations on arriving at the Growing step! Get ready, this is when we throw jet fuel on your brand and you start to explode and take off! It might not come immediately, but it will come, I promise you. Stay the course and buckle up.

This step is all about growing your database of existing and potential customers, building campaigns to speak to the pain points your potential customers have, and even branching out of your reach with targeted paid advertising.

Check for yourself, tech overwhelm is a serious concern

Before we jump in, let's talk about tech overwhelm. The options are endless because they are. Every year Chiefmartec.com releases a new chart of the marketing technology landscape, categorized by:

· Advertising & promotion

· Content & experience

· Social & relationships

· Commerce & sales

· Data

· Management

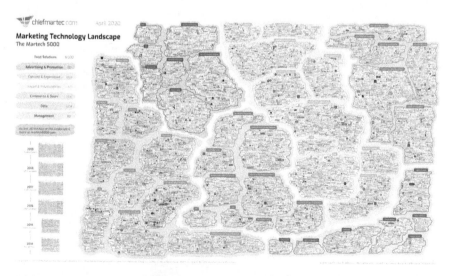

Holy cannoli, this is a lot, right? Believe it or not, inside each section are brand logos of current software solutions available on the market.

Here's a closer look at just the CRM section. (Remember to breathe!)

Wow! That's overwhelming all on its own!

There were 947 software options in 2014. As of the 2021 publication of this book, there are now more than 8,000!

Finding the right software to help streamline your process is becoming more and more accessible to the masses of small business owners.

However, evaluating and testing solutions can become a full-time job. AND software subscription fees can start to chew into your bottom line and increase your overhead.

Instead, see what comparable competitors in your industry are using to try to piggyback off of their research.

I don't have a solution for evaluating the best software for your business needs, other than trying it out, but my main point here is to normalize the overwhelm and help you stay focused.

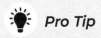 **Pro Tip**

*It's better to get started with software that is 80% effective at solving your needs over spending an absorbent amount of time trying to find the **perfect** solution.*

CHAPTER 7

CUSTOMER RELATIONSHIP MANAGEMENT

Nurturing the list of your tribe can generate constant business.

One Thing I Wish I Knew 20 Years Ago

Who is the easiest person to sell your product or services to? Someone who has already bought from you.

That's why it's SO NECESSARY to track your customers' contact info.

Your list is gold

Growing your customer base through Content Relationship Management (CRM) software is key to nurturing your clientele and growing sales. We'll work together to define your lead generation spigot: a way to reach your target audience and continue to grow your customer base over time.

There are many options that can be part of your growth plan, including content creation for YouTube, social media, paid ads, email marketing, and search engine optimization. Our final step in the growth phase is to build your first campaign, giving your audience one clear solution to a problem they're facing.

At this step, you are striking a balance between closing sales, fulfilling orders, and maintaining quality. Everything within this chapter, and frankly this book, is connected, which is why it is so important to UNIFY it.

Starting out

To track your customer list, you can start with a spreadsheet. Anyone else feel triggered by just seeing that word? Don't run away just yet! It can be as simple as including customers first and last name, email address and physical address, if applicable. Keep it simple, but be sure to track! As your client base grows, however, it is beneficial to use CRM (Client Relationship Management) software. This allows you to take more of a hands-off approach to managing

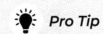 **Pro Tip**

Your business is so valuable that you can only interact with your customers once! Structure your business to offer services on an ongoing basis to better support your customers and generate a more steady income. Examples of this include packaging products, offering follow-up services, maintenance plans or memberships.

client data, keeping your customer information secure and easy to access. Benefits also include analytics, email marketing and simplified list management for personalized outreach.

Software Solutions

CRM tracks your customer contact information and helps you reach out to segments of your audience all at once in bulk.

Large companies

There are big CRMs like Salesforce and Hubspot, which are for larger companies with big databases (think hundreds of thousands of subscribers) and a steady stream of content delivery. These are awesome, robust CRMs, but you will end up paying for features you do not yet need as a smaller business.

Medium companies

With tens of thousands of monthly email subscribers, ActiveCampaign, Klaviyo, AWeber, Drip and Keap are great options for businesses to look into. These platforms aren't free, but offer functionality that will benefit your slightly larger audience, with room to grow.

Starter CRMs

For start-ups and small businesses, MailChimp, Constant Contact, or Vertical Response are fabulous options. They are affordable, scalable, and generally offer a free plan to get up and running. You can always use your database to export it and move it to another platform as you grow.

Figure out how many emails you want to be able to send per month, how many audience segments you have, the capabilities you want included and then do research on potential solutions.

Test drive a few options before finding the right software, as they are all a bit different and you might enjoy a workflow or user interface more than another.

CRMs often offer analytics that track metrics for your email open rate, click rate, and suggest actionable insights to increase your engagement rate. Keep an eye on what is working and what hasn't resonated with your viewers.

Email Campaigns

What is an email campaign?

When we talk about email campaigns, it is, at its core, just sending one email to a bunch of people at once. I'm sure you are very familiar with receiving these emails from retail brands you have purchased from.

We call them campaigns, because they are thought out prior to sending "targeted" specifically to the viewer reading them.

Email campaigns are sent from a CRM or Customer Relationship Management software with your specific database of friends, customers, fans, members, etc.

So why use CRM to send bulk emails?

One major reason you don't want to just email your list with your general email address and carbon copy them or blind carbon copy them is that your email provider will get flagged as a spammer and lock or drop your email account. Yikes!

Why you need email campaigns

The BEST thing about email is that you OWN the list. It is yours. Unlike social media, where you are limited by the almighty algorithm which will limit your ability to reach all of your followers, (only something like 4% of your followers on Facebook see your post in their feed). However, with your email database, you can reach all of your readers as long as you follow best practices and stay out of their Junk folder.

Another reason to focus on email is that it is active and not passive. An email will go and grab your potential customers in their inbox as opposed to a potential customer having to be compelled to reach out to your website.

There are varying strategies and tactics for sending emails out to your database.

How to make it most effective

Experiment to see what yields the best results for your business and audience. There are text-based campaigns (like an email you receive from a close friend) or campaigns that are obviously from a business or organization that include images, colorful buttons, and embedded video.

Text-based options are good if you want your email to feel personable as if it is coming directly from you. The image-based format is great if you want a design that is more formatted like your website, or you want to feature a photo, product image, video, or content that you want to visually organize.

Choose a list, segment, or tag

You can send a campaign to a group of people on your list, a segment of your list, or even a tag that you have used in their profile. For example, if you have a list of "Oil Change Customers" you may send them an automated email once they purchase from you with a follow-up email reminder from 90-days.

Or you might just have a segment of that list that needs their tires rotated, so you can segment your list into just customers that need to receive an email about tire rotations, why we need to do it, and how to order that service from you.

And a tag can be a way to "tag" them in your CRM with something they are interested in, like "interested in easy diy" because they downloaded your lead magnet on "Tips for checking your tire pressure in the winter." Then you know to send them an email reaching out to them about how not to hassle with checking their tire pressure in the cold, and just buy your tire services from you.

Create or choose a template

You don't have to select one and feel stuck to it forever. Instead, choose or design a template for the majority of your email campaigns that is unified and reflects the look and feel of your website. Every once in a while when you have a more personal message, send a text-only email and see if that elicits a different response.

Branding

Use your hero image or at least your logo at the top of your email template. Integrate your brand colors, fonts, and additional images. It doesn't have to look like an exact copy of your website, but using these defined elements from Brand Step #1 builds brand recognition and authority. You want to be memorable!

Email Campaign Launch Checklist

Here is a checklist of items you'll need when sending out a campaign:

☐ *Campaign name*

☐ *Which list do you want to email to*

☐ *Which layout do you want to use*

☐ *Do you want your subject line to be*

☐ *Which emojis do you want to use in your subject line*

☐ *What copy should you use for your preview text*

☐ *What images or videos to use for your content*

☐ *What copy to use in the body of the email*

☐ *What your call-to-action button should say and link to*

☐ *Make sure your landing page is public*

Preflight checklist

Send a test before you publish to the public to check for spelling, check all links, and ensure you have an enticing CTA!

When to publish: days and times

There isn't really a hard and fast rule to publishing content, but generally speaking it is better to spread content publishing out evenly rather than just dumping a bunch of content into your feed or bombarding someone's inbox. Find what works best for you and review your analytics to see which times drive the most engagement.

For me, I would never post on a Friday afternoon about marketing a business, because many business owners are wrapping up for the weekend and getting out of "work mode." But, if I owned a pizza joint, publishing on Friday afternoon would be essential because people have worked all weekend and just want to not have to think about prepping food and grab a pizza for movie night.

This is all to say, be strategic about what will work best for you based upon what your viewer needs or will be most engaged with your material.

Drip out your content

One type of email campaign is Drip Sequence, which we will talk about more in depth later in this chapter. A drip sequence is a series of emails gradually giving the reader more information over time.

Test to see what works

Something fun with email campaigns is the ability to run different tests to find the best results. For instance, you can test different subject lines, call-to-action wording, change the title of your lead magnet or the graphics you use to show off that freebie. You can try out the different variables in your emails to see what works best and track results within an excel doc or Trello to keep everything in one spot.

Don't be intimidated by the concept of testing and analyzing. An easy way to begin is to divide your contacts in half and send one group, one subject line and another a different subject line. After 3 days, take a look at which email was opened by more customers.

Then look at that subject line and figure out what might have enticed the customer to click. Was it personalized? Did you use emojis? Was the wording more fun? Gamify the process and have fun!

Metrics to consider when reviewing a campaign:

· What was your open rate?

· How many people unsubscribed?

· How many people clicked on your CTA?

· How many people bought from your website?

Lead Generation

Finding new potential customers is key to growing your company and diversifying your customer base.

> *"Lead generation is the process of attracting and converting strangers and prospects into someone who has indicated an interest in your company's product or service. Some examples of lead generators are job applications, blog posts, coupons, live events, and online content."*
>
> *HUBSPOT*

Lead Generation can be a tough nut to crack. In this section, we'll cover growing your database by defining and nurturing your lead channels. A lead can show interest in your product or service by email, text message, word of mouth, direct message, over the phone, or through a fill-in form on your website.

The goal is to take this stranger and convert them into a paying customer by leading them through a nurturing process. Marketing circles often compare this process to dating. You don't just walk up to a total stranger and propose marriage to them. Well, most of us don't anyway. You "nurture" the relationship over time. First, you might meet for a coffee. Then dinner. You let the relationship bloom organically.

Sales should be more of a commitment in your relationship. You're eventually looking for loyalty, which is like marriage.

But of course, we're getting ahead of ourselves here.

The first question is: how do we attract the right people that are most likely to buy from us? How do we find these perfect matches?

This is where the work on your ideal client in Step 2: Defining comes in. Go back and look over who your target customers are so you can "show up" where they hang out, speak to their biggest business problems, and offer a FREE solution.

Zoinks! Gee, Shaggy, did you say, FREE?! How am I going to run a business if I give it away?!

Well, they do pay. With the currency of their contact info.

Lead Magnet: Show Them What You Have to Offer

One way to convert a stranger into a lead is to offer a FREE piece of content. There is a value exchange here - their contact info for your content. So whatever it is you're delivering should be valuable to your prospects. It can be:

- PDF download
- Exclusive video
- Webinar
- Online Course

This magical exchange should be beneficial for both parties. Your visitor gets to "test drive" your content, your likability, and communication style. You get the opportunity to serve them, provide value, possibly sell your product or service to them, and bring value to their lives.

What if they don't like you? Great news! If they don't find value in what you offer in your lead magnet, there are two opportunities:

1. Get feedback to shift your content; or

2. You both see that person isn't your target customer and you can refine your outreach.

LEAD MAGNET	
SOLVES A PROBLEM	Buyer Persona
PROMISES QUICK WIN	Download Checklist Cheatsheet
INSTANT ACCESS	Download Checklist Cheatsheet
REFLECTS YOU	You are the expert. Give them your expertise and they will return.
FREE TRIAL	No Credit Card
VALUE	You won't keep them if you don't understand them.

Creating a lead magnet can attract your ideal customer. Here are some ways to catch their attention.

After that, the goal is to have a handful of high-quality lead magnets you can advertise, either paid for or organically through social media, as well as to your current database. This will separate the wheat from the chaff, and you'll be able to speak even more nichely down to this group of people.

A lead magnet is what will invite your web traffic to exchange their email for some valuable free information (that you do not have listed anywhere else otherwise this would defeat the purpose). It needs to be valuable and concise. Trust me, no one wants a 50pg eBook. They'd rather have 3-5 pages of to-the-point, high-value information. This will also ensure they trust you up front because you are offering them something without asking for any compensation.

If you are unsure how to create your first lead magnet, use a tool like Canva. There are many free templates on the site that can be altered as you see fit to create a visually pleasing and easy to read PDF. Oh, and it's free.

Lead Magnet Examples:

- *Our top 10 recommendations for (something in your industry)*
- *Checklists for how to master (something in your industry)*
- *3 reasons you need (product or service) in your life*
- *10 things that could be stopping you from (addressing a pain point)*
- *How to (solve their problem) in 10 easy steps*
- *How I (do something that they can't) and get massive results*

Notice any similarities to these titles? They all tell the reader EXACTLY what they can expect to learn. That's a title-approach you can bring into email subject lines, blogs, and tutorial videos. Just make sure you deliver on your promise.

Lead magnet automation: focus on what is important

When it comes to your business, automate anything you can. Even better if that automation comes with personalization. The right software will do both of those things.

Your CRM software should have the ability to automatically send your lead magnet to your prospects as soon as they sign up for it. The CRM will have its "how-to" and you'll have to do a little bit of front work.

1. Write an automated email

2. Embed a bit of code into your website.

When someone fills out the form to access your freebies, your CRM will send an automated email with the download link or access information. Having this automated is really helpful.

First, because people are really used to receiving their lead magnets immediately. They want a solution NOW. Like yesterday. So if you take too long, they're moving on.... to your competitors.

Second, you don't want to receive an email every time someone signs up for your lead magnet and then have to send them a custom email. This is not a great use of your time.

Automation for drip email sequence

Another impactful automation is a drip email sequence. It is called a "drip" sequence because one email, containing information about a certain topic, gets sent (dripped) out on a schedule you decide upon.

The whole reason a reader signs up to receive your emails is because they want to learn more or make a purchase.

If your drip sequence is not relevant, they will no longer open your emails or unsubscribe altogether. According to Jupiter Research, they found that relevant emails drive 18x more revenue than broadcast emails, so staying relevant to your audience is key to your marketing success.

Beyond being relevant, according to Instapage, personalized email marketing messages tend to generate an average ROI of 122%.

This is where your CRM can provide incredible value as you can use your list segments to personalize emails to users based on their age/interest.

The number one reason people unsubscribe is that they are over saturated with emails from a single sender and could even report you as a spammer, which can hurt your sending results over time.

According to Keap.com, you should send an email campaign from as little as once a month to up to once a day, if your offer changes enough to provide value.

Utilize this technique to roll out a "welcome sequence" to new subscribers or new customers.

When someone signs up for a free resource, a drip sequence might look like:

1. "Welcome!" email

One day later (as designated in the CRM)

2. Company founder introduction. This develops trust in the relationship building cycle.

One day later (as designated in the CRM)

3. Introduction to main offering.

Three days later (as designated in the CRM)

4. Invitation to download more free resources to build relationships and assist you in developing groups within your CRM to better reach out to that individual.

Three days Later (as designated in the CRM)

5. More in-depth about product offerings and a reminder to take action such as an online quiz.

Three days later (as designated in the CRM)

6. Emotional draw. Speak directly to your customers and the problems they may be experiencing. Email is "personal outreach" to book a time to chat directly in case they are feeling overwhelmed and just want to talk with a human and get direction.

A few ways you can use drip sequences are:

- Welcome campaigns
- New customer onboarding
- Shopping cart abandonment
- Recommendations
- Renewals and confirmations
- Education

The goal of a drip sequence is not to overwhelm or smother the viewer with everything you want to tell them, but deliberately guide them through the process of learning from your brand.

Let's go ahead and put this into practice! Think about how you will utilize a drip sequence through the examples below.

DAY ONE

Subject line: Here's your _____ guide!

Message: Welcome! Here's your free resource!

Goal: Deliver the goods.

DAY THREE

Subject line: _____

Message: Thanks for downloading your resources. We hope you've found it helpful. I'd love to introduce myself.

Goal: Build rapport and trust.

DAY FIVE

Subject line: A deeper dive into _____

Message: _____

Goal: Give prospects a deeper understanding of what we offer and how we can help them

Offer a CTA at the bottom of each email to show the reader what they should be doing with the information you have rolled out to them.

Here are some dos and don'ts of email drip campaigns:

Do:

- Map out the logical flow of your content before building your drip campaign.
- Consider the waiting period before sending the next email.
- Send at least 3-5 emails in your sequence to offer a nice flow of information over a period of time that is comfortable for your viewer to digest.

- Make each email small and digestible for your audience to read, and take action on without getting overwhelmed.

- Display the action steps they can take to move forward with the information you've displayed in your email.

Don't:

- Bombard your viewer with content or just ask them to buy from you over and over.

- Send boring emails that lack substance or content.

- Just send a few emails on your drip and think that it is going to be of a lot of value to your viewers.

- As with any campaign, don't make your emails too text-heavy or overloaded with graphics. Keep it simple and easy to digest.

Here is an example of what my drip sequence could look like:

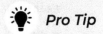 **Pro Tip**

Keep your content quickly digestible and space out your delivery to find balance between offering help and keeping your brand top-of-mind in their inbox, but not to anchor them down and overwhelm them with tasks.

Lead Magnet: Invest in the Best 5-Day Course

EMAIL ONE

Subject line: *[Day 1] Invest in the Best Course*

Message:

Welcome to Day 1 of the Invest in the Best Course!

KNOW WHAT & WHEN TO HIRE OUT

Today we'll talk about why you need to hire help and why you can't build a business alone. We'll also talk about tips for who your next first (or next) hire should be, what are some possible positions to hire first, the stress of letting go as a business owner, and how to do it with success!

Goal: *Watch video*

CTA: *Watch Day 1*

EMAIL TWO

Subject line: *[Day 2] Invest in the Best*

Message:

Welcome to Day 2 of the Invest in the Best Course!

How to know what you don't know & writing a clear job description.

Today we'll talk about how to reverse engineer job descriptions that need to be done in our company, even if we know nothing about them.

We'll talk about conducting research, defining your terms and desired outcomes when writing your clear job description, and talking about your company's mission only if it is worth hooking people.

Goal: *Watch Day 2*

CTA: *Watch Day 2*

EMAIL THREE

Subject line: *[Day 3] Invest in the Best*

Message:

Welcome to Day 3 of the Invest in the Best Course!

WHERE TO POST JOB OPENINGS OR WHERE TO LOOK FOR THE RIGHT TEAM MEMBER

Today we are going to talk about trying to find the right platform to post your job to attract the right people.

We talk about these contractor websites:

Fiverr, Upwork, Indeed, Freelancer.com, Handshake, Glassdoor, Belay Solutions, Zirtual.

Goal: *Watch Day 3*

CTA: *Watch Day 3*

EMAIL FOUR

Subject line: *[Day 4] Invest in the Best*

Message:

Welcome to Day 4 of the Invest in the Best Course!

STEPS FOR FINDING QUALITY CONTRACTORS

Today we are going to talk about sifting through applications and resumes and how to get to a YES. Then we talk about how to set up interviews for your top 5 picks and build rapport.

Goal: *Watch Day 4*

CTA: *Watch Day 4*

EMAIL FIVE

Subject line: *[Day 5] Invest in the Best - Final Class*

Message:

Welcome to Day 5 of the Invest in the Best Course!

HOW TO MANAGE CONTRACTORS

Today we are celebrating our new contractor with lots of positive feedback and our reclaimed sanity. We'll also talk about how to communicate expectations and maintain relationships.

Goal: *Watch Day 5*

CTA: *Watch Day 5*

Even if they read or viewed your lead magnet, diving deeper into each subject can bring more value to your viewer, and then at the bottom of each drip email, you can offer additional services or products for sale.

✏️ EXERCISE   DRIP SEQUENCE

Lead Magnet: _____

EMAIL ONE

Subject line: _____

Message:

_____

_____

_____

_____

Goal: _____

CTA: _____

EMAIL TWO

Subject line: _____

Message:

_____

_____

_____

_____

Goal: _____

CTA: _____

EMAIL THREE

Subject line: _____

Message:

_____

_____

_____

_____

Goal: _____

CTA: _____

EMAIL FOUR

Subject line: _____

Message:

_____

_____

_____

_____

Goal: _____

CTA: _____

EMAIL FIVE

Subject line: _____

Message:

_____

_____

_____

_____

Goal: _____

CTA: _____

⬇   Download a copy of this worksheet at UnifyYourMarketing.com

As you can see, despite the bad rap it can get, lead generation is really just one more way to let your creativity shine. Figuring out what your customers are looking for, delivering a solution and building rapport to keep them coming back is a skill that will benefit your business tenfold. With the right balance of value, enthusiasm and interactions with your ideal customer, your business will thrive!

CHAPTER 7

KEY TAKEAWAYS

Customer relationship management

- Software Solutions
  - Tech Overwhelm
  - Software Solutions
- Email Campaigns
- Focus On Lead Generation
  - Determine Your Lead Magnet: Offer
  - Set Up Your Lead Magnet: Automation
  - Create Your Email Drip Sequence

CHAPTER 8

CAMPAIGN INITIATIVES

Increase awareness and generate sales through a product or service that is defined by time.

Alright, I'm pumped. Building campaign initiatives is one of my very favorite steps in this whole dang process. It is fulfilling to identify a customer problem, provide a solution, give that whole process an identity, and turn it into a full-blown campaign. We're surrounded by campaigns everywhere we look, but only the best make an impact.

A campaign initiative is creating an identity for a product or service that is defined by time. For instance, you could design a campaign initiative around an upcoming holiday sale, or a new product launch.

This campaign can be deployed through print and digital vehicles like print ads, video, social media, website pages, cold calling, and email campaigns.

One main goal is to increase awareness and generate sales. The bigger the campaign initiative, the greater the reach and the more sophisticated the scope of the campaign. However, you want to be mindful of not over-doing it. Sending out too many campaign emails is a quick way to unsubscribe and you don't want that.

You've seen lots of campaign initiatives before

Think about it in terms of a political campaign. These are some of the premiere campaigns in the world, and we get to see them rolled out every few years when someone is running for president of the United States.

Beginning with a name, the campaign is branded. They create slogans like, "I'm with Her", "Change We Can Believe In", or the infamous "Make America Great Again." Then there was the logo that was used on a myriad of political ads, stickers, campaign posters, and yard signs in all the correct brand colors.

Politics aside, "Make America Great Again", as a marketing campaign, was incredibly effective. It was recognizable, easy to remember, and evoked emotions from the viewers. All the ingredients needed for a successful campaign.

The campaign who made the voters the hero won

You know back in the Brand Script chapter we talked about how we want to position our viewers as the hero of their own story and us as the guide to help them become the hero.

Well, this theory prevailed right before our eyes when we saw the election campaigns of 2016, and so let's break down the structure of their slogans for just a moment.

"I'm with her" implies that she is the hero and we are attaching ourselves to Hillary Clinton. While "Make America Great Again" implies that we as voters can be the hero of the story by our own action of voting for Donald Trump. Maybe there might have been a different outcome had the campaign slogans positioned the voters as the hero on both sides. We'll never know, but it is a reminder that how you say your messaging, and from which perspective you say it matters.

In Donald Trump's 2016 presidential campaign, "Make America Great Again" positioned the voter as the hero of their own story.

While Hillary Clinton's 2016 presidential campaign, "Hillary" positioned her as the hero, which led to fewer votes.

Other familiar campaign Initiatives

When we are talking about creating a campaign initiative, think about an upcoming season, like a Black Friday Sale or Mother's Day sale. How many times have you heard some women's voiceover work say "Mother's day is right around the corner and you should give her something she'll always cherish...."

Or my wife's absolute favorite, and I say this completely sarcastically, is the Lexus December to Remember sale. Every year we see a gigantic red bow on the roof of a shiny new car with one partner buying a car for the other partner as a surprise for Christmas.

My wife would be SO mad if I ever did something like this for her. And yet, they must work, because they use the same campaign tactic year after year. Long story short, a high-quality campaign can be an effective way to help get your message out to raise awareness or generate sales.

Your Next Campaign

Now YOU get to have the fun of determining your first campaign. Creating a campaign is as simple as starting at Unify Brand Step #1 and going through the process again but this time, it's focused on one particular initiative. See how the Unify Brand Steps are repurposed to drive the campaign below:

Campaign Step 1: Defining. Brainstorm individually and then with a small team of trusted advisors to nail down your initial concept.

Campaign Step 2: Building. Take your initial concept comps and pitch the campaign to your team. With a few graphic elements designed, you can present a well defined campaign to your whole team and get them excited to jump on board!

Campaign Step 3: Growing. Create an offer or lead magnet around your campaign to grow your audience. This will be your main energy going into launch day!

Campaign Step 4: Ongoing. Ride the launch day enthusiasm as you work on your content pipeline and schedule (with deadlines!) new content for the campaign.

Campaign Step 5: Scaling. Analyze and track what is succeeding and keep doing that! Deliver great customer service, fulfill your orders, and continue to grow your campaign.

Campaign Step 1: Defining

It's time to get your team excited for the campaign! To start, involve a small group of trusted advisors to begin brainstorming with you to kickstart the concept.

When in a concept meeting you share with your team:

- What the campaign is about
- Why it is needed
- How they can help
- Ask for any feedback
- Get their buy-in BEFORE you nail down the concept

Work together to define your brand script for this campaign. What amazing offer can you create? How can you generate excitement about a new product or service? Think about what would make your customer want to jump up and take action to be sure not to miss out?

Name that campaign

You don't have to have a catchy slogan to achieve a successful campaign, but you DO need to come up with something that gets people to pay attention. You can see (and hear) examples of "sticky" and memorable slogans all around you each day.

See if you can remember these famous campaigns:

- Maybe she's born with it
- Where's the beef?
- Because you're worth it
- Breakfast of champions
- Melts in your mouth, not in your hand
- Can you hear me now? Good.
- Quicker Picker Upper
- America runs on Dunkin'
- Like a good neighbor, ___ __ is there

It might be just as easy as the name of your product if it is something distinguishable from other products. If it doesn't work, try to give it a name that is identifiable.

NO cell phone	NO mop	NO laptop computer
YES iPhone	YES Swiffer	YES Chromebook

If it is a service, try and work to create something that is memorable. "Cleaning Service" isn't really catchy enough. But "Spring into Clean Bundle" or "Spring into Clean Savings" has more of an identity to it.

Keep an open mind

There are usually awesome ideas generated from those around you who have differing viewpoints or skill sets. Be willing to listen to and consider a bunch of terrible (often laughable!) ideas but continue to push forward as you never know what will spark the perfect inspiration.

I have found that sometimes offering up a wacky idea that I know is awful not only lightens the mood but boosts the willingness of others to share. If the meeting goes off course, keep the enthusiasm but move the team back to discussing the main goal of the campaign.

After your brainstorming sesh, take some time to let those ideas marinate before moving forward. Weed through the ideas and see what stands out. Hopefully you have come away with some high quality concepts as well as a list of hurdles you may have to work through with the help of your team.

Share your revised list of ideas with your trusted advisors and get their feedback again before taking it to the larger group. Your goal is to nail down a concept that the larger team can help you flush out in the look and feel.

 Pro Tip

Remember this is brainstorming! Let it be fun and off-the-wall, you never know where something might lead. Take notes on a large white board or screen to keep everyone engaged as they see their ideas validated and appreciated. Your team's enthusiasm will help carry you through the campaign as well!

Bring it to life

Once you and your trusted advisors have agreed upon a final concept, make it come to life with graphic elements before you pitch the concept to your whole team. You may only need one or two elements to present on the pitch so don't worry about having the designer flush out every last detail but you want your team to have a feel for the campaign. As an added bonus, this helps you see all your brainstorming come to life and keeps you energized!

Campaign Elements

Title of the campaign: _____

Visual identity

    Fonts: _____

    Campaign colors: _____

    Hero image: _____

Value proposition: _____

Call-to-action: _____

Campaign Step 2: Building

Pitch your revised campaign to your whole team

Once you have a few graphic elements designed, it is time to present a well defined campaign to your whole team and get them excited to jump on board!

Present actual campaign mock-ups from landing pages to social media and print postcards. Your advisors will experience the campaign through your audience's eyes and ears. Ride with your team member's enthusiasm!

The goal is to talk about the problem you need to solve, your solution, why your company is poised to offer that solution.

Ensure your team members that you've considered the extra work a campaign can create as well as solutions in your well thought out timeline.

Outcomes to share with your team through the pitch:

- The problem
- Your solution
- Campaign name (with styled graphics)
- The campaign hero image
- Campaign video (optional)
- Landing page mockup
- The call-to-action
- Campaign timeline

As a business owner, you're enthusiastic and love your business. Having your design concepts thought out and polished will go a long way in helping your team capture your vision for the campaign. Stoke the small flames within each of them, helping the fire and passion for the project to grow!

Determine your timeline

Often, the best campaigns can take months to conceptualize, create and execute. Beginning with your launch date, work backwards to determine a realistic timeline for production. Take feedback from your team on how you can best support them throughout the launch. After solidifying your launch timeline, assign a lead for each task, schedule check-ins and determine what success looks like if you're able to meet your goals.

Use the Unify Launch Sequence worksheet that we use to track tasks and roles for 6 months from concept through and then after the campaign launch. Begin by determining your launch date and work backwards to set deadlines throughout. You will also want to make space for any follow-up work after the launch of your campaign for analysis and future recommendations.

Assigned team responsibilities

Next, assign each team member their tasks in creating the visuals and written copy that will define your campaign. These assets will be the leading impression of the entire initiative, so make sure all design

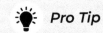 *Pro Tip*

The more energy you have behind a campaign with you, your team, and your raving fans, the more successful your campaign will be. I've never heard of a campaign that was launched quietly and was very successful, so get everyone on board and excited.

elements use the exact same colors, fonts and general feel. With these assets you will then be able to build a landing page, which is a specific page on your website just for this campaign that might not look like the rest of your website but has all of the visual identity elements from your new campaign.

Reference the list below to ensure you have the assets created to update all your channels to match your campaign. Remember to Unify all of your marketing with this particular initiative's identity for the greatest impact.

Campaign Launch Checklist

- [ ] Campaign landing page
- [ ] Website home page
- [ ] Social media channels
- [ ] Email signature
- [ ] Window clings
- [ ] Clothing
- [ ] Freebies/giveaways
- [ ] Promotional videos
- [ ] Digital video ads
- [ ] Digital image ads
- [ ] Print ads
- [ ] Email campaign template

Campaign Step 3: Growing

At this stage, work on creating a lead magnet around your campaign. Offer free content in exchange for someone's email address, and continue to reach out to them during the campaign.

Launch day!

Launch day can be nerve-wracking. You never know how things will take shape and be received by your target audience. Will you have quick success? Slow and steady sales? Or dead in the water? If it is the latter, don't hesitate to pivot, or push with more energy. Sometimes patience, listening, and data can help get you out of your slump, so collect as much of it as you can.

Campaign Step 4: Ongoing

Work on your content pipeline and schedule (with deadlines!) new content for the campaign. A good campaign will have 7-10 customer touchpoints so define a strategy for what they are before the campaign begins. Also, assign team roles.

Campaign Step 5: Scaling

Analyze and track what is succeeding and keep doing that! Deliver great customer service, fulfill your orders, and continue to grow your campaign. After some time you will begin to see your ROI grow. Review your sales numbers. You don't want to spend money you don't have, so start small and make sure your ad works. If not, adjust as needed before spending more money to push it out to larger audiences.

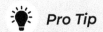 *Pro Tip*

For every new campaign, make sure to update your website, social media, in your email campaigns, and print media with this new campaign identity.

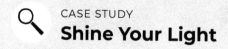
Business-to-Business Donation Initiative

Client: *Hanley LED*

Company Description: *Commercial signature illumination solutions.*

Pitch/Concept/Challenge: *An end-of-year fundraising initiative. 1% of HanleyLED sales were donated to the Children's Miracle Network.*

HanleyLED's campaign goals included:

· Donate 1% of their sales in December

· Raise more funds for CMN

· Drive more LED unit sales by the end of the year

· Incentivize internal salesforce to focus on LED unit sales

HanleyLED, a B2B company, sells LED lights to sign manufacturers and installers to illuminate commercial signs.

Think of any sign above a restaurant, gas station, retail store, etc. If the sign was lit at night we wanted HanleyLED to be the lights used inside it.

You see these signs all over the place. Think Cracker Barrel, Starbucks, or Shell stations. Those huge three-dimensional signs out in the parking lot that you can see a mile away all have lights in them to illuminate them at night.

 Pro Tip

Invest in marketing. Upfront investments (i.e., printing and shipping costs) pay off with higher profits, increase their first-time customer base, and make substantial donations to CMN.

The hero image for HanleyLED's SHINE YOUR LIGHT campaign. Shown here is the poster design that was displayed around their 50+ locations.

Shine Your Light

Creative process

With my team at Unify, we decided not to highlight "1%". First, it sounds like a small number. Second, I had no interest in associating with the "one-percenters" aka the super-rich political puppet masters. We had to think of a campaign name that would be well received and memorable.

A great philosophy, popularized by Donald Miller of Storybrand, is to show off and empower the customer as the campaign's hero (rather than the selling company). The lighting element of HanleyLED is also a unique design opportunity we want to incorporate.

Out of the 30 campaign concepts, the winner was: "Shine Your Light".

The "Shine Your Light" Campaign invited the customer to be a hero to the children and families supported by Children's Miracle Network.

We know the campaign was successful not just because of the uptick within the month of the campaign but also over time as their sales numbers continue to grow. Consider both of these metrics to consider when calculating your ROI on any investments you make into the campaign.

Shine Your Light

"Donation thermometer:" We designed a poster that was manually filled in as sales/ donations grew for each branch across the country. We adapted the typical fundraising thermometer to the Children's Miracle Network balloon logo. Using this element made the concept more cohesive and enforced the idea that you weren't just selling more LEDs, you were helping more children.

Freebies: Branded giveaway items are always a hit. Customers enjoy them and they keep the campaign initiative at the forefront of their minds. Plus, they're basically real-life influencer marketing. We designed our give-away items around the December winter weather. One was a coffee mug and the other was a winter beanie, both of which HanleyLED customers used and enjoyed.

Not every campaign will be a home run. Remember the Twitter riot from the 2017 Pepsi Kendall Jenner ad, or the 2010 launch of a new logo signature for the Gap retail store, which lasted 6 days after internet upheaval? Adjust and move forward.

Huddle up team time to track our key metrics

Once you have launched, the next step is to follow up with your team, get feedback on what is working and what needs improvement, and learn as much from your first launch as possible so you can apply what you have learned for the next campaign.

Don't just launch and disappear. Keep up the energy with your team. They will take care of the external customers.

Follow-up with your customers, get their feedback, and let your team know in a post-campaign briefing meeting.

Key Metrics to Track

- Number of units sold
- Number of customers who purchased
- Number of first time purchasers
- Number of customers in your database before the campaign
- Number of customers in your database after the campaign
- Website views during the campaign (growth in percentage)
- Cost of the campaign
  - Staff
  - Contractors
  - Advertising costs
  - Printing
  - Design
  - Any additional costs associated with the campaign
- Gross sales
- Return on investment percentage
  - Cost of the campaign - gross sales = profit
  - Profit / cost of the campaign x 100 = ROI percentage

Example

If you spend $5,000 on the cost of the campaign and made $15,000 in gross sales, your ROI formula would be:

15,000 - 5,000 = 10,000

10,000 / 5,000 = 2

*2 x 100 = **200%***

At the end of that briefing, schedule the next campaign kick-off meeting. Keep it going!

Max Metal's Max Madness

Business-to-Business Sales Initiative

Client: Max Metal

Company Description: Manufacturing company.

Campaign Goal: Sell 30,500 units of 4'x8' sheets of aluminum within a month.

Pitch/Concept: Max Madness

Before the high tariff on aluminum was to take place at the turn of 2019 between China and the United States, our client, Grimco, a sign manufacturing supply company, purchased as many shipping containers of aluminum as they've seen in a long time.

They bought 15x the normal order. They hoped that with the higher demand and a solid marketing effort, they could ship some units to their customer base and attract new customers.

They contracted me to guide their marketing department through the process of delivering a solid campaign. This was an audacious goal. Fifteen times more?! Are you kidding me?!

After regrouping and trying not to be psyched out by the staggering number, my team guided the marketing department through the process of producing a streamlined campaign to sell like crazy!

Since this campaign was during March, we decided to have the theme based around March Madness, the NCAA basketball tournament. Combining March Madness with Max Metal, the campaign was called "Max Madness." We used basketball imagery as part of the visual identity for both the external messaging as well as the internal sales competition.

The marketing team at Max Metal did a great job of creating quality visuals to brand the campaign, and there was plenty of energy provided by leadership to get everyone involved aware and excited about the event.

Did I mention that we have one month to deliver results?

Max Metal's Max Madness

The shipping containers were on a boat in the middle of the Pacific Ocean headed for Long Beach, CA, where they would be transported by rail to St. Louis, MO. Time was not on our side, but we were focused and the team moved fast.

The campaign kicked off really well.

Email campaigns, website landing pages, social media blitzes, and sales calls were all part of the initiative to flip these units.

Just two weeks into the campaign, we had sold every single unit! CHA-CHING! Not only that but they gained 690 first-time purchasers! Needless to say, they were thrilled with the results.

The Grimco office dry erase board in the marketing department was a thing of beauty!

CHAPTER 8

KEY TAKEAWAYS

Understanding campaign initiatives

- Create your next campaign

- Campaign Step 1: Work with a trusted team of advisors to define your brand script for this campaign.

- Campaign Step 2: Build out the campaign and share it with your whole team. Determine the launch calendar and define team roles.

- Campaign Step 3: Grow your campaign through an enticing lead magnet and successful campaign launch.

- Campaign Step 4: Manage your ongoing campaign post launch day, managing content creation and deployment.

- Campaign Step 5: Analyze and track what is succeeding and keep doing that! Deliver great customer service, fulfill your orders, and continue to grow the campaign.

- Follow-up with your customers, get their feedback, and connect with your team for a post-campaign briefing meeting.

Was it fun brainstorming together and strategizing what might get your customers excited? I hope you had a chance to laugh with each other over a few outlandish ideas, spurred some new creativity and broke the ice with your team. Campaigns can be fun, energizing and inspiring, not to mention lucrative in the long run. Now that you have your first campaign launched and analyzed, let's explore how you can share your solution with a wider audience.

CHAPTER 9

EXPAND YOUR REACH

Cast a wide net and share your business solution with the world.

CONSIDER HIRING A CONTRACTOR

Networking

We've all heard the saying about "it's who you know not what you know", and this is just a reminder that if you don't get out there and meet new people, nobody will know about your business. Networking is an awesome opportunity to tell your story, what you're excited to do on a daily basis, and find more people to help. That's what this is all about, right??

3 Things to know about networking

1. *Make networking work for YOU:* What are 3 things you like about networking? Write them out and figure out what kind of networking events or style might fit you best. We all know we avoid things we don't like so don't let that be what stops you from networking. Find a style that works for you!

2. *Networking can be fun:* Whether one on one or a large networking event, you get to decide the direction of your conversation. You don't necessarily have to be direct or salesy, in fact it can be purely fun to learn about others, have a good conversation and realize you're not alone in some of the struggles of owning a business.

3. *Mi casa, su casa:* It might not be that the individual you're working with is your client, but as you talk, it may become more obvious that someone they know, or someone you know might need what the other is offering. Taking the time to learn about their business, what they struggle with or others they know that might be looking for a solution you offer can lead to some really fruitful conversation. While it may be a one to one conversation it can quickly expand to be about your entire networks and how they might intertwine.

Meetings with personal contacts can be an amazing way to reignite your passion and stoke your sales fire to bring in new customers. I found each of these things to be true through an exercise I dubbed 30 Coffees in 30 Days.

Networking challenge: 30 coffees in 30 days

I want to challenge you to get out there with your business and take your brand script and shop it around to people that need your service. I want you to book 30 appointments and grow your network. Create some momentum. Get the energy of our business going! So here is how we are going to do this:

- Create a list of 10 people that are your most likely to buy your new offer from you, that you know.

- Send them all a personal message, or hell, even give them a call on your cellular telephone, (gasp!) and take them out for coffee.

- Once you meet, ask them about their business and really get to hear their successes and pain points.

- Ask them, "How can I help?" and truly see if you can help them.

- They will in-turn ask how they can help and you can mention your offer and ask them if it is something that they are interested in pursuing.

- Then ask them who they know (in their network) who could use your offer. Get names and contact info and even ask for an introduction.

- Work to fill the remaining slots over the next month with people outside your network.

- You can "advertise" your challenge to your network via email, social media, word of mouth and start to book slots as much as you can. Get after it! Where your attention goes, energy flows!

- Create a graphic to give this challenge an identity, like I did with the cup. You can use the graphic like the proverbial thermometer to illustrate that you are reaching your goal.

- Follow up the meeting with a thank you message and follow up with any solutions that you have for their pain points.

- Keep them and their pain points in mind as you move about life and try to solve their problems and get back to them with ideas. Goodwill goes a long way.

Ways to expand your network

Here are a few great spaces to explore networking opportunities:

- Clients
- Family, friends & neighbors
- Local business community
- Events/conferences
- Chamber of commerce
- Local networking group
- Social media groups
- Resources to expand your offerings

Public Relations

Advertising is something you pay for. Publicity is something that you pray for.

Publicity over advertising

Getting into other people's networks is one of the fastest and most effective ways to grow your audience. It is also an incredibly cost-effective way to gain publicity, build your company's reputation and gain client trust.

By gaining publicity, you can also gain "social proof" where your clients are willing to speak highly of you to their networks. For example, if you manage a yoga studio, the most valuable sales tool is a client leaving your class and telling a friend, "I am so excited because I finally found a yoga studio where I fit in." Their friend can see their glow and wants that same experience so they look you up and book your introductory class. Publicity is like magic, but far more rewarding and attainable and doesn't cost you ANYTHING but taking care of people.

Beyond taking excellent care of your current customers, here are a few ways to infiltrate new audiences:

· Start a referral program to thank clients when they refer someone to you

· Ask clients for testimonials (Refer to Step 2: Building)

· Collaborate on a presentation or webinar with someone whose audience you want to get in front of

· Be active in your local community

· Be a podcast guest

· Be interviewed for a blog or newsletter

· Write a piece for the local newspaper or an industry magazine

· Feature other content creators on your channels

Publicity for my film

When I was working to premiere *Paving The Way*, I wanted to do it in my hometown of Davenport, IA, part of the Quad Cities, where all of my family could come and celebrate with me.

My dad understands the power of publicity and reached out to the local newspapers, radio, and TV stations and got me on a local magazine TV show, interviewed for a radio program, and featured as a big event happening in the weekend paper. All of this, along with his enthusiasm for word-of-mouth advertising, packed every seat of that 350 seat IMAX Theater that night. We even had to turn a ton of people away! That night the local news station came and featured the premiere and the sold-out show as a segment on the ten o'clock news.

It was another huge example of the power of publicity. Thanks, Pops! Thanks for being my #1 cheerleader. Love you!

Organic marketing

Throughout this chapter we've been talking all about different types of organic marketing. Gaining publicity through reaching out to your personal network and the networks of those you know IS organic marketing. You are getting your company's name and mission out into the community at a relatively low cost. That is the key difference between organic and paid marketing. Organic marketing is anything you can do that expands your reach but doesn't directly incur any costs to your business. Now, that does not make organic marketing free. You will pay through your time, efforts and even occasionally coffee or lunch with a prospective client. But you will also more often have a much higher ROI due to the personal nature of the relationship.

Content marketing

As we discussed in Step 2, creating additional content for your website will help further the value it provides. The Content Marketing Institute, an online resource for information on all things content marketing related, defines content marketing as a marketing technique of creating and distributing valuable, relevant and consistent content to attract and acquire a clearly defined audience – with the objective of driving profitable customer action.

 Pro Tip

In my experience, the more PR you can get the better, so work towards getting as much exposure as you can! Reach out to PR specialists or do some guerrilla PR to get your story out to people that are looking for content and specialists to interview and publish on their platforms to their networks.

When we talk about content marketing, we are talking about:

- Webpages
- Infographics
- Podcasts
- Videos
- Books
- Art
- Webinars
- Templates
- Blogs
- Articles
- White papers
- Case studies

The buying cycle

Before we get into what content marketing is, it's important to understand why content marketing is beneficial to your business.

To do this, we need to understand the four steps of the buying cycle:

1. *Awareness.* Your customer may have a need, but they are not aware there is a solution.

2. *Research.* Once aware of a solution, the customer often performs research to educate themselves. For example, a person looking for a car will look at what cars exist and which ones might fit their needs.

3. *Consideration.* As they become aware of their options, customers will begin to compare products to ensure they're getting the best solution to fit their needs at the best price.

4. *Buying.* Finally, after some research and consideration, your customers make the move to move forward with their purchase.

Content marketing is the perfect way to help people in the first two stages of the buying process by raising awareness of solutions and educating consumers about a product they may have never considered before. However, in order to be considered, your content first needs to appear when a customer searches for you!

Pro Tip

As a videographer, I often begin my content marketing efforts with a video, from which I can turn the transcript into an article, multiple social media posts, and even a free download. This may differ for you, depending on what you love to do, but just ensure you're consistent.

Continually generating new content for your website, and social media is KEY in building authority in your market.

The #1 secret to content marketing

Add value. Yup, that's the secret! Customers will skip advertising when it provides little to no value. It's not really a secret at all. If your content speaks to your customer or addresses an issue they might have, they won't skip it.

YouTube has perfected this algorithm. You will notice that if you watch a lot of wood working or home improvement videos, the ads within your videos will be for tools and other equipment you may need. You will soon find yourself completely enamored with a video advertising a kreg jig to help you create a more polished end table and walking out the door to go get one because you realize it's something you MUST have to complete the project. Content marketing at its finest!

If your business solves a problem, you have ample material for content marketing. Begin to brainstorm what you find fascinating about your business that others might not know. Put yourself in the shoes of someone looking for what you offer and imagine what search terms you might use to search for a solution. Then, base videos, articles, podcast episodes, etc. around those topics.

The number one goal is to consistently post new content on your website, social media channels and any other outlets, to build a very robust web presence with lots of relevant information that benefits both your visitors and your SEO. If you're adding valuable content, you'll find yourself with a tribe of supporters who are grateful for your expertise in no time!

SEO and content marketing

According to HubSpot, 75% of searchers never go past the first page of search results that come up — this is why it is so essential to rank on the first page of Google.

Search engine optimization (SEO) is how companies position their site to show up first on Google, Bing or other search engines.

Despite the acronym, SEO is as much about people as it is about search engines themselves. It's about understanding what people are searching for online, the answers they are seeking, the words they're using to find answers, and the type of content they wish to consume. Knowing these answers will allow you to connect to the people who are searching online for the solutions you offer.

To determine the relevancy of a page (SEO) search engines use bots (also called crawlers or spiders) to scour billions of pieces of content and evaluate thousands of factors to determine which content is most likely to answer your query.

All of this is done through discovering and cataloging all available content on the Internet (web pages, PDFs, images, videos, etc.) via a process known as "crawling and indexing," and then ordering it by how well it matches the query in a process we refer to as "ranking."

SEO is all about including essential information updated and accurate across all sources (like your location), placing #keywords that visitors use when they're searching (i.e. emergency pest control), and producing consistent content that speaks to your area of expertise (a blog named "How to raise chickens without inviting mice over for dinner" with photos). That way, when someone searches for "emergency mouse exterminator near me," your business shows up on the first page of results.

There are a number of techniques you can use to build out both the frontend and backend of your website so your content is indexed in search engines and your customers can find you, easier.

According to SEM Rush, here are some of the elements to focus on to grow your website traffic and visibility:

1. Align your content with search intent

2. Write a compelling title tag and meta description

3. Optimize your images

4. Optimize your page speed

5. Use internal linking

6. Improve the user experience on your website

7. Include keywords in your URL

8. Focus on getting more authoritative backlinks

9. Publish long-form content

There are lots of great resources on the web as well as books to help you learn about search engine optimization, but there are also lots of professionals who can help you achieve your SEO goals. Don't shy away from spending money on an expert to make money!

1. A few resources I recommend:

2. Anything by Neil Patel

3. Moz.com

4. SEMRush.com

Recommendations for finding an SEO specialist

When looking for an SEO specialist, ask them for results that they have gotten for other websites, and ask them for recommendations and the process of what they would do to your site to make it more SEO friendly.

When you talk with an SEO specialist, ask them about the elements we outlined above with the elements to focus on to grow your website traffic and find-ability and what you can do to boost this information on your site.

Also, when you are done having the site optimized, don't forget to continue to build out more content that fills the void that people are searching for online. The more dense and rich with keywords you want to be known for the better the chance that you'll be found online easier.

Paid Advertising

Digital ads

If you haven't done any paid advertising yet, I'd advise that you start with digital advertising, because you can track your data clearly, and test what works before you move to a medium that is harder to track. If you want, start even smaller such as with social media ads like on Instagram or Facebook (since they're the same company).

You can put out ads for as little as $5/day and track analytics to see what's working and what isn't. This is a great way to soft launch a test campaign before you spend money on a larger commitment.

Paid advertising requires a lot of time, attention, and financial resources to test, adjust, and prosper.

I appreciate the hell out of data, but not the most analytical person when it comes to collecting data and analyzing it. It isn't my power zone. Instead, I rely on the professionals and internal team members to grow our company with paid advertising.

Hire a contracted ads manager to start

Paying an outside contractor should not be a set-it and forget-it hire. Educate yourself so that you can participate in the process overtime. The best way to do that is to partner with ad buyers who are willing, and dare I say eager, to demystify the world of paid-ads. Seek to understand strategy, best practices, target audiences, and whatever else they say is a significant factor to success.

Find an ads manager with the heart of a teacher

According to Marketo.com, there are six metrics to follow when tracking your digital advertising campaigns:

- *Impressions:* This shows you how many times your ads have been served. In other words, the number of people who have seen your ads.
- *Clicks:* The number of people who have clicked your ad after seeing it.
- *CTR:* Click-through rate of impressions to clicks as a percentage.
- *CPC:* The average cost-per-click across a campaign.
- *Quality Score (AdWords):* This is used by Google to measure the relevance of your ads to the keywords you're targeting. Factors include CTR, landing page quality, and relevance of the keyword to the ad and search query.
- *Relevancy Score (Facebook Ads):* A score from 1 to 10 that measures how relevant an ad is to its target audience.

In an interview I had with Josh Anderson, the owner of Active Tide Marketing, I asked him what we should be looking for in paid ads and the said, "It depends on your overall goals. So, if you are interested in top of the funnel – awareness/traffic/email signups – then I would really focus on Cost Per Click, on conversion rate (if going for email signups), and cost per conversion. You can have a great CPC but if you aren't converting then it's for naught.

"This also means that I recommend you have a dedicated action you want your traffic to take once on your page. Strong calls to action are important.

"Of course, if you are doing just a 100% brand awareness and recall play, you will want to focus on cost per impressions (a cost that you pay when your ad is shown per one thousand impressions) and ad recall (a metric that shows how memorable your ad is to your audience).

"Now if you are going for more lead generation, in the middle of the funnel campaign, like Facebook Form Fills, you really need to focus on Cost Per Conversion (Form fill in this case).

"Ideally, for both instances, you'd like to set up your campaigns to determine your cost per conversion which you can tie a dollar amount to so that you can determine your ROAS (return on ad spend)."

How do I know if an ad is working?

When you can, correlate your ad spend with sales. But maybe not exactly the way you might think about it.

Your ad spend might be a $1 per one new customer purchase of $15. That is an amazing return. But what if you spend $20 per new customer? Seems like a loss, but how often will that person come back and spend t $15 or more the next time they need your solution?

Consider your ad spend cost versus the total lifetime value of that customer. For instance, you might have to spend $500 just to get one customer, which might sound like a lot, but if your industry is financial advisory, and the lifetime value of that customer is $1,000,000, that is a mighty fine investment, right?

This will help you to figure out your ROI and whether or not the money you are spending on an ad is not only evening out (which it absolutely needs to) but becoming profitable, too. You need to be sure your ad is not draining money, but rather bringing new money in to pay for itself and more. That's why every element of an ad campaign must be considered carefully. Additionally, you need to consider who to push out your ad to and when.

So, how do you calculate your lifetime value of a customer?

Having sales data is very important here. But, generally, if you get a customer to purchase from you, and let's say that they buy a membership to your coaching program, it costs $100 per month.

And you know that on average each member pays their membership dues for 18 months, then you know the life cycle of your average customer is $100 x 18 = $1800.

You will have some people stay longer and some shorter, but on average they currently stay 18 months. You can work later on the retention rate, but for now, you know that you have $1800 as your anchor.

So, now you know that you FOR SURE need to keep your advertising costs under $1800, or you aren't making ANY money.

The goal is to get a new paying customer for as little as possible, but tracking your ROI (return on investment) is key to growing and scaling your advertising and business profit.

The goal is to put $1 into paid advertising and get at least $3 back.

You can define and set your own goals with your ads manager.

Print ads

With the growth of digital media you may think Print Ads aren't nearly as effective as they once were -- But, research shows consumers trust print ads 34% more than search engine ads. In fact, print advertisements have a significant impact on converting prospects to customers. Nearly 80% of consumers act on direct printed mail advertisements compared to 45% of consumers that act on electronic advertisements.

We all get mailers from the local dentist, landscaper, politician, or even local big box store. They wouldn't keep sending them to you if they didn't work, so there is proof that they keep bringing people in!

Print ads include:

- Billboards
- Magazine ads
- Newspaper ads
- Postcards

Let's look at some beautiful print ads and examine what is working for them. What does their actual ad look like? What message are they trying to convey? Is this something that you could emulate and pull off for your brand?

Three different post card designs using styled logo signatures, hero images, and hierarchy that displays the most important info biggest and at the top and the details smaller and toward the bottom.

Elements to include on your next print ad:

☐ *Eye catching & authentic image*

☐ *Prominent message*

- *Highlight viewer's pain point*
- *Highlight success if they work with you*

☐ *Value proposition*

☐ *Event date, time & location*

☐ *Accreditations, awards, certifications to build credibility*

☐ *Call-to-action*

☐ *Contact info*

☐ *Deadline - what is their reason to act now?*

Tracking effectiveness with print ads

While print ads are one of the more difficult to track, there are some great ways to ensure you can track your ROI.

1. The best way to track the effectiveness of a print ad is by creating a specific print campaign. This campaign is strictly used for print advertisements, tailored to be effective in print format. Go through the steps in Chapter 8 to define and create your print campaign.

2. With any successful campaign, you will want to create a specific landing page on your website for your print ad. Keep it super simple and memorable, like yogastudio.com/freeclass so that you are able to know and track who signed up for the class after seeing your print ad.

3. Finally, your campaign should have a custom coupon code for customers to check out with. Make sure the coupon code is prominent on the ad and only used within that print advertisement campaign. That allows you to know that the person who used the coupon saw your ad and it was effective in driving a sale.

In the end, print ads can be an incredibly effective way to reach a new audience. While tracking can be a bit more cumbersome, stay consistent and intentional and you will find what works for you. Your efforts will pay off!

CHAPTER 7

KEY TAKEAWAYS

Expand your reach

- Paid advertising is beneficial if done correctly.
  - Hire an ads manager and partner with them to learn how paid ads can best serve your business.
  - Public relations: getting into other people's networks is one of the fastest and most effective ways to grow your audience.
- Search engine optimization: connect to the people who are searching online for the solutions you offer.
  - Hire an SEO specialist to boost your SEO and teach you how to continue to grow your brand reputation online.
- Content marketing: creating additional content for your website will help further the value it provides.
  - Ensure your content adds value for your customer.
- Print ads: consumers trust print ads 34% more than search engine ads, use them strategically to continue to add value.
- Networking: personal contacts can be a long term way to bring in new customers.

Whew! Does anyone else feel like they've run a marathon? Working through so much and absorbing new information is simultaneously exhausting and absolutely exhilarating. You may have hit the proverbial "wall" a few times, but you've made it through and conquered Unify Step 3!

Now that you've been able to create a way to grow your business, it is time to work on what work should be done on an ongoing basis to maintain your effectiveness in running your company.

UNIFY STEP 4

ONGOING

Determine your content production pipeline, team roles and schedule content to maintain a top-of-mind place in your viewer's attention.

01
DEFINING

02
BUILDING

03
GROWING

04
ONGOING

05
SCALING

With a clear mission and targeted solution from Steps 1 through 3, it's time to show you exactly how to produce content that is:

- Valuable
- Consistent
- Engaging
- And shared across all of your channels

This is where you define your campaigns, creators, editors, and publishers. Produce a content calendar to layout topics, production schedules, and assets.

The goal is to create content once and run it through your content production pipeline. This will allow you to make the most of your time and effort so you can save time and money moving between designers, photographers, videographers, web designers and social media managers all while delivering consistently valuable messages to your viewers.

Consistency is key

To become an authority in your industry you must publish content consistently if you want. This is non-negotiable. It's what will set you apart from the crowd. Social media is an endless sea of pictures, videos, captions and information. Whether you've been in the game for years or are just starting out, it's going to be difficult for people to see you as an authority in your field without seeing consistent content that allows people to easily see what you're all about.

Your Brand Script defines your business niche and ideal customer. Now it's time to figure out what type of valuable content you're going to produce and create a schedule you know you can stick to.

Creating content can be an extremely hard thing to do, especially when running a business. However, people perceive you as an authority BECAUSE you publish content. You need to have a plan early on for how much content you are going to create.

> *"Being known will beat being the best every time."*
> *GRANT CARDONE*

There is a finite amount of attention for each potential customer and the whole point of doing this work is to be top of mind! Let's move into Chapter 10 to figure out how this works for your business.

Growing your audience

"Everybody starts with zero f*cking followers."

GARY VAYNERCHUK

I also want to mention for a minute here that like Gary says, we all start at zero. If you are just starting out, you won't have a big list, and if you have a big email list, but are just starting out on YouTube, you have to start at zero.

I have grown lists, audiences and followers for different niches over the last few decades and one doesn't carry over to another, and each one is custom to your particular business. It is part of the DNA of your company.

Only your business has this specific combination of fans, clients, customers, subscribers, followers, and that is something you should be proud of.

But it isn't easy to build an audience. It takes time, patience, and consistently showing up for them.

The bigger your audience the better your chances of being a successful business owner, so focus part of your time on reaching people who need you and nurturing that relationship.

When you follow the Unify Brand Steps, you will be a rockstar in your industry and it will be hard for people to ignore you. Go get 'em! You got this!

CHAPTER 10

DETERMINE YOUR CONTENT PRODUCTION PIPELINE

Build a repeatable system to create, deliver and track content.

The goal of Step 4: Ongoing is to figure out how to create and deliver ongoing content to your clients and prospects, so you continue to offer value to them even after you've sold them your product or service. In order to do that, let's take a look at your current team work-flow.

Audit your current situation

At the outset, we all have great expectations. We have grand visions for our website and social media feeds. We imagine how inspired our clients will be to receive our monthly newsletter. Then the reality of running a business and publishing regular content feels like walking through molasses.

So how do we reduce overwhelm and keep providing valuable content? Begin by figuring out what your team is already doing and build from there.

Team roles

Survey all of your team members, ask them what parts of the content production pipeline they work on, and map it out. Now, most companies don't think of what they are doing as part of a "content production pipeline," but jot down who:

· Comes up with the ideas

· Writes articles

· Edits

· Website content updating

· Taking photos

· Print material designing

· Video shooting & editing

· Social media posting

Once you complete your audit, you'll have a better understanding of where your team's energy is focused. It will give you insight as to how to direct them in the future.

Let's take a look at a real life example of this in action.

Communication Flow

Company: *Good Shepherd Lutheran Church*

Industry: *Religion*

Size: *1,500 members; 10 staff*

Goal: *Redesign an outdated website*

Challenge: *Communication breakdown between content creators*

In working with Good Shepherd Lutheran Church, the goal was to update the website to make it feel more like the in-person worship experience. The person in charge of the site consistently updates it with relevant content, so it just needed a new look and feel.

In the process of building their site, it became clear that there were several staff members with their hands on different communication pieces.

Over the course of a few weeks, those who contributed to various communications pieces included:

- The Head Pastor
- The Associate Pastor
- The Youth Pastor
- The Director of Family Ministries
- The Deacon
- The Bookkeeper / Communication director
- Admin Assistant #1
- Admin Assistant #2

There are many different content pieces including weekly bible lessons, church group announcements, volunteer opportunities, event updates, and prayer requests, small group activities, etc. that have to be broadcast every week and the staff's job is to make sure all the members know about all of these things.

Communication Flow

The struggle was that often, the left-hand didn't know what the right hand was doing. The individual who is responsible for emailing the congregation didn't tell the person who designs the weekly printed insert, and the person who manages social media posted the incorrect date on Facebook.

This communication struggle happened all of the time and it really wasn't anybody's fault. The communication flow was too interrupted and therefore stalled out in certain places. You can see the disjointed communication flow in the chart below.

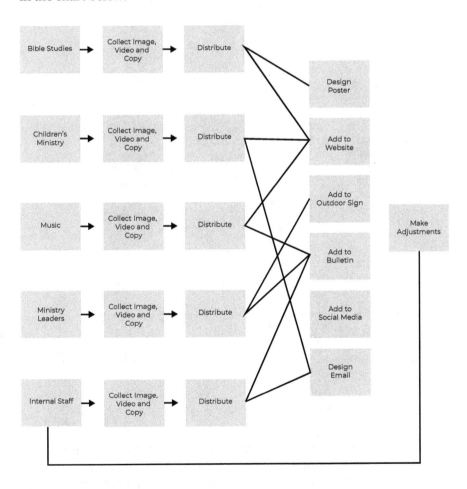

The disjointed communication flow.

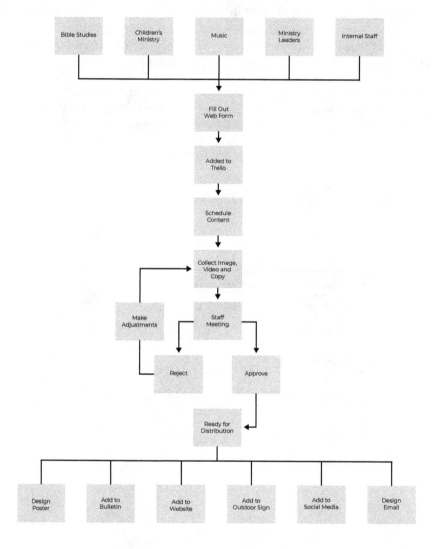

The streamlined communication flow.

As you can see, the updated communication flows through the pipeline and is distributed to all of the different communication channels like mass emails, social media, print newsletters, and website updates. There are far fewer boxes in their redesigned content production pipeline because we cut out redundancies and streamlined tasks.

Communication Flow

The staff helped organize the flow by task, and not by person. We directed everyone to submit their news requests through an online form that asked:

- Name
- Event
- Event date
- Event description
- Call-to-action
- Contact person
- Contact email
- Contact phone

The form triggered an automatic email to the Director of Communications. Once approved, it was forwarded to the first person in the content production pipeline.

Using their project management software, they can track each submission and make sure it moves down the production pipeline and is distributed everywhere. It was a frickin' miracle to see this rolled out and working in action.

It saves a ton of time, energy, and stress when it comes to building and running your business. The ability to add team members, delegate tasks, and check on their status will save you so much in the long run and the basic version is totally free to use.

The outcome was that every touchpoint to our members was a consistent message no matter how they interact with the church.

Hallelujah, Jesus!

Content Production Pipelines

So, what exactly is a content production pipeline? It is the order in which you publish and distribute your content. It is the workflow you define for your business and then assign to your team, so it is disseminated and tracked everywhere you possibly can.

Pro Tip

Your team may already be working through a content production pipeline that has not yet been defined. Writing down and formalizing the process and who is responsible for each step will ensure you're not missing out on opportunities to share with a larger audience.

You will only need to define your content production pipeline once but will use this same process every time you publish a new piece of content. Your team will know how to support you because it will be defined and you will save your sanity because you don't have to do it all.

Defining this pipeline is essential to making sure you share your content on every platform. For example you want to take any content that you publish to your website, but if you aren't sharing it on your social media channels your audience on those platforms won't get to see it.

Or if you end up publishing a deal on your social media page, but not developing a landing page to secure that deal on your website it might be harder to track and those who go to your website will miss out!

Here is an example of a content production pipeline that could be used for a company that wanted to focus on written content.

Sample Content Production Pipeline

1. Team brainstorm of content ideas	2. Team member writes up best idea	3. Produce images/ illustrations	4. Copy is proofed
8. Posted to the website	7. Content is approved for distribution	6. Feature image is created	5. Send to content manager
9. Posted to Facebook page	10. Posted to LinkedIn	11. Designed in Mailchimp	12. Monthly reporting

Define your own content production pipeline

Let's determine what your content production pipeline looks like!

Grab a sheet of paper and jot down your own 12-15 steps that are required to get a piece of content out to the world. Imagine you are filling in the boxes on the chart above.

- Where do you begin generating ideas?
- What would your ideal work flow be to ensure your content is getting out everywhere with a system that will run smoothly time and time again?
- Once you have come up with the steps of your own content production pipeline, take it to your team to cross check any steps that may need to be added.
- Start with ideation or topic ideas and end with archiving or monthly reporting to circle back on what is working and what missed the mark.

Once you've defined your content production pipeline you won't have to create it again, but continue to use it as a guide to walk you and your team through the process.

Here is an example of a bullet point content production pipeline:

- *Brainstorm content ideas with team*
- *Outline talking points in Google Doc*
- *Record video*
- *Upload files for editor*
- *Review and approve*
- *Send to Rev to transcribe*
- *Edit down into short clips for social*
- *Post audio to Anchor.FM for podcast*
- *Post all to website*
- *Schedule posts on HeroPost*
- *Analyze results*

It doesn't have to be fancy, just functional!

Make it once and put it EVERYWHERE

The beauty of a content production pipeline is that once you create something, it won't be a one-trick pony. When you publish an article, helpful graphic, or how-to tutorial, you will have a plan for how to customize the delivery message for every platform audience you speak to. The way you tweet is very different from the way you address your monthly newsletter followers. You need to nuance messaging in order to penetrate your distinct audiences' attention, but the concepts can be the same.

You also want to consider the different ways people consume information. Some people like video, some prefer to listen to podcasts and audiobooks, others read books and articles.

Experiment with how you create and deliver content. Track how a written blurb engages your audiences compared to a photo with text over it, or the way a video tutorial is received alongside the same content crafted as a how-to article. There is no one silver bullet here. It all depends on how your audience likes to receive your content.

Give each project an identity and track the publication process

This system can easily be applied to any company in any industry. It's versatile enough to use for general YouTube channels, order fulfillment, and businesses of all shapes and sizes. Whether you're flying solo or have a large team at your back you can benefit from using these tools to help you streamline workflow processes within your business.

Let's look at Red Meat Lover's internal tracking system. As I mentioned earlier, we use an online platform called Trello. Within the site, users can create their task boards with different columns and move the tasks between them.

 Pro Tip

Thinking about how customers would find you is a great way to align your content with what people want to find. Think about what they would search for, the pain points they might Google, the service they might be looking for, place they live, etc.

Typically columns include task statuses such as To Do, In Progress, Done. Red Meat Lover has a board, or one unified spot, where all information is housed. Everyone on the team has access to it. Within that board, there are cards designated for each video project or content piece.

You can also write checklists, assign tasks and due dates, and write notes to one another within each card. This helps track conversations and anyone at any time can see what's happening. It also helps you if you need to manage revisions or re-assign things. It's a lot easier than having a list on a digital note or something else, trust me.

The system runs chronologically in columns from left to right, from ideation to delivery or publication. Users complete their task for each card and move it forward right down the line. Each board starts with an idea column that we can always pull from when we're looking for new content.

Here's a visual of a Trello Board with content moving down the queue. This setup shows what's in the queue and who needs to work on it, giving us a wide-angle view of production.

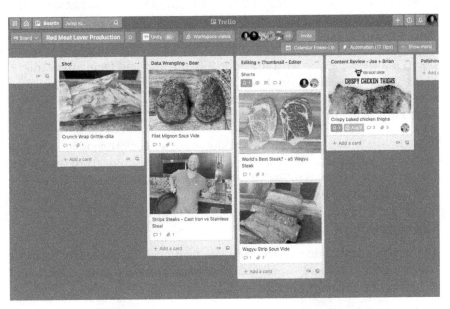

Here is our working Trello board for Red Meat Lover, and you can see that each project has a photo and working title that we can keep track of during the production process.

Project Management in Action: Red Meat Lover

In working on Red Meat Lover, we have learned a great deal about optimizing the content we create. When we shoot videos, we will make sure we're able to do 3 to 5 different videos in one shoot.

The editing process begins when I assign it to an editor within our team board which gets it into the production pipeline.

With the videos in the pipeline for editing, I go through the photoshoot and make sure I have any additional photos that we might want to add for social media, blog posts, and newsletters.

Thumbnails

We use images for the thumbnail on YouTube, images for our blog posts, and social media. You can use a free program such as Canva to create Instagram posts, book covers, YouTube thumbnails and so much more. This is another great tool you need to be utilizing early and often in your business when it comes to consistent content creation.

Each thumbnail needs to be eye-catching, clickable, enticing. Be sure the photo is a clear picture with someone looking into and facing the camera. You want eye contact and a smile if possible in this still. It should be something that captures your audience and makes them feel invited to click on the image to learn more about the video.

If the image is unappealing, they're not going to click the video. Think of it like a virtual book cover. I might have additional photos from the photo, from the video shoot. I might've taken photos in this case of food or of Joe cooking and of the ingredients.

Written copy

The written description of the video or transcript of the episode can be used for blog posts and social media posts, giving us a plethora of content from just one day of production work.

Scheduling upcoming content

In an ideal world, you are developing a pipeline of content in advance that you can schedule out in advance. Hopefully you even align your content with the calendar year (for example, Holiday Gift Guide, or Father's Day

Sale, or Valentine's Day Sale, or Superbowl, March Madness or Kentucky Derby).

Whether it's your website, email software, or social media, there are ways to frontload your content and schedule the date and time it is published. This means you can produce more when you're in your slower times of the month and have that ready during the busy times of month— or when you want to go on vacation.

Distribute to social media

And then from there we ship it out to the social board, which is a whole other board about sharing on social media. This board handles the workflow and assignments of each task to publish to our website, Facebook, Instagram and to our email subscribers.

CHAPTER 10

KEY TAKEAWAYS

Consistency is key

You must publish content consistently if you want to become an authority in your industry.

Define your content production pipeline

This is the workflow you define for your business and then assign to your team, so you don't have to do it all.

- Generate many content ideas at once to improve efficiency
- Case study: tips for content production pipeline scheduling
  - Pre-production
  - Shoot day
  - Post-production
  - Delivery
- Analyze your team roles and map out your plan for delivering content consistently.
- Case study: a streamlined communication flow can save you a whole lot of time, energy and headache.
- Project management in action: Red Meat Lover
  - Thumbnails
  - Written copy
  - Scheduling upcoming content
  - Distribute to social media

HEYO! WE'RE ROLLING NOW

You've discovered the beauty of creating and delivering **ongoing** *content to your clients and prospects, so you continue to offer value to them even after you've sold them your product or service. Your analysis of your team roles will not only help everything run more efficiently but keep frustrations between team members at bay (win/win!) Let's keep moving to figure out exactly what kind of content you can create that is most valuable to your customers.*

CHAPTER 11

CONTENT CALENDAR AND SCHEDULE

Solidify your authority in the industry by publishing content consistently.

Have you ever set up a social media account, email newsletter, or blog, published for a few weeks, and then abandoned ship? Guilty! It can be daunting and overwhelming, can't it?!

A great way to surpass this road bump is to map out your content in advance. Some people do a week in advance, others do months. The more you do ahead of time the less you'll have to do later which saves you a lot of time, and stress!

What matters is that you stay consistent with whatever schedule you decide on so your audience knows when to anticipate new content from you. Think of it this way. If a podcast or YouTube show you loved came out completely randomly, how would you anticipate making time to watch or listen? It would be hard to remain a fan of something that is inconsistent.

But before we get moving forward with building out our content schedule, let's go back to talking about delivering valuable content.

HARD STOP: value is more important than frequency

As discussed in Step 3, the #1 secret to content marketing is to deliver valuable content to your audience. Your content needs to have value. You can't just post a photo with some hashtags and expect people to care.

Likewise, you can't make posts that are all about you all of the time and expect people to care. While sure, it's interesting to learn about your journey or why you're an authority figure in your chosen vocation, people care more about what you can offer them than what you can say about yourself. Think back to the fitness example.

The currency of business is attention

Let's say you're a mom who wants to lose weight. You want a female trainer, preferably even one with kids because she'll know your struggles first hand at losing baby weight. Are you going to feel like you connect with male trainers who are bulky gym bros? Likely not. What about the ultra-fit supermodel trainer who has 10% body fat and never had a baby and is known for her intense hour long workouts? Nope.

Then she finds a trainer who promises quick, easy, at-home workouts (great for busy and tired moms) in 30 min or less. The trainer is a mom herself and struggled and succeeded at losing baby weight and promises she can help you, too. Bingo. That niched down trainer just landed her ideal client by being specific and offering targeted value.

If you aren't top-of-mind with your audience, there is a very good chance that they will find another voice/business/solution besides yours. With that, you have lost your ROI, and all of your other efforts have been for naught.

Publishing content consistently presents you as an authority

As we discussed in Chapter 9 regarding SEO and Content marketing, consistently publishing content gives your SEO a boost as you are adding more ways to be found in search engines and consequently by your ideal audience.

As an added bonus, having more content out there adds social proof validating your authority.

Strategize your content release schedule

As stated at the beginning of this chapter, it's better to do less with more value than to overdo it with low-value content. That's a quick and guaranteed way to lose followers and followers equals business.

Pace your content with consideration about your audience and how much value you are bringing them and set up your calendar accordingly.

Once you assign a campaign concept to the pipeline, assign the publication day, and then work backward. Leave some room for contingencies, like team members being on vacation or tied up on other projects.

Look at a calendar and find a good launch date that is in the future by at least a month away, to get started, and then, you can start to fill in the production schedule and strategize on content ideas.

By having it a month away, it gives you time to stay ahead in creating content. It also gives you margin in

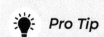

Pro Tip

"What gets scheduled gets done." When you schedule in your content, you are setting yourself up for success in actually creating content and staying consistent. Subscribe to this philosophy, hold yourself accountable, set a schedule and stick to it!

your time, so you don't get burnt out, and leaves room for when you are out on vacation or buried in a project. This also provides a layer of safety in the event you get sick or need to deal with a life event such as a family emergency.

The last thing you want to be worrying about is your content schedule. Do it in advance, and you won't have to think twice no matter what comes up in life.

Using a Content Calendar

I highly recommend that you use a calendar to schedule content ideas, creation time, review periods, and due dates because it is a great way to stay organized and launch valuable.

See the example below highlighting how content is scheduled out for upcoming social media posts.

Content Schedule

1 (Sept 1-14)	2 (Sept 14-30)	3 (Oct 1-15)
Why this book? Why now? What are the steps?	Let's Get You a Quick Win	Foundational Work

4 (Oct 15-31)	5 (Nov 1-15)	6 (Nov 15-30)
Step 1: Defining	Step 2: Building	Step 3: Growing

This is just an example of what your content calendar could look like. This is a basic outline of what topics we want to promote for this book launch!

Some benefits of keeping content calendars include:

· Remain current on trends and important dates

· Insert guest bloggers as needed

· Prevent unnecessary time gaps between posts

· Organize creative assets

- Reduce stress
- Manage your time

The easiest way to schedule upcoming content is to think about the frequency of your publications.

Are you publishing every hour? Every day? Week? Month? And then dial it in; every hour at 15 mins after the hour, or every day at 1pm, or every Tuesday, or on the first of the month.

How to Generate Content Ideas

So, how do you identify content that is valuable to your audience? There are lots of different ways to get the ol' creative juices flowing, but the key take-away of this section is to understand your ideal customer.

When you understand your ideal customer, you can speak to the problem they are encountering which then builds trust and confidence in your expertise. Trust and confidence in your product or services leads to sales.

It is also vital to keep up with current industry trends and standards to most effectively meet your customers where they are and reach new markets.

Research is the key to better understanding your customers and what they are looking for. Here are some ways to stay in-touch with content ideas:

- Read blogs
- Subscribe to emails
- Follow other industry leaders on social media
- Network in your industry
- Attend trade shows
- Listen to podcasts
- Read books
- Survey your customers

This research can generate oodles of content ideas.

EXERCISE GENERATE CONTENT IDEAS

Here Are 15 Ideas to Generate Content

Grab a notepad and start jotting down ideas. You are in the hot seat, let's start the clock!

1. *Create topic lists in bunches.* Create an ongoing list of possible content ideas and review them often.

2. *Social media followers.* Poll or survey your followers for their pain points.

3. *Blog comments.* Review your blog comments and see if that sparks something for you to write about.

4. *Conduct interviews.* Interview specialists in your industry.

5. *Competitor websites.* See what your competitors are writing about.

6. *Google search suggestions.* In the search bar, start to put a keyword in and see if it finishes the sentence and sparks an idea.

7. *Recent events.* Can you relate current news events or holidays to your content.

8. *Product reviews.* Can you review a product in your industry or highlight a review that has been created about your product or service?

9. *Topic generator platforms.* Go to HubSpot blog ideas generator and get some inspiration.

10. *Personal stories.* What personal stories can you tie to your product or service?

11. *Sign up for newsletters.* Sign up for other industry-related newsletters to gain some inspiration.

12. *YouTube videos.* Search YouTube for what is there or what might be missing and fill in the gaps.

13. *New products and technology.* Are there new products coming to the market or new technology that is industry-related?

14. *Use data and analytics.* Use data to tell a story.

15. *Revisit previously published content.* There might be an update needed, or to come at the concept from a new perspective to tell a better story.

When finding topics to generate content about consider these as a starting point:

- *Ask your readers/viewers a question.*
- *Show a tutorial about something that would help them out.*
- *Go behind the scenes*
- *Conduct an AMA (ask me anything)*
- *Share valuable thought leadership*
- *Conduct an interview with an industry leader*
- *Jump on a trend*
- *Feature user-generated content*
- *Create a photo collage*
- *Use a daily hashtag to spark inspiration*
- *Share your mistakes*
- *Show a before and after*
- *Share an action shot*
- *Show an influencer using your product or service*

EXERCISE   CONTENT PILLARS

Create Your Own Content Pillars

Take some time and map out your main content pillars or the core topics that you are going to center all of your content around.

Once you have your ideas generated, it is time to create your content calendar and schedule out your content.

1 Topic:	2 Topic:	3 Topic:
Description:	Description:	Description:
4 Topic:	5 Topic:	6 Topic:
Description:	Description:	Description:
7 Topic:	8 Topic:	9 Topic:
Description:	Description:	Description:
10 Topic:	11 Topic:	12 Topic:
Description:	Description:	Description:

✎ EXERCISE   CONTENT PLANNER

Content Planner

Here is a content planner to help you plan out one post or piece of content. Here you can pick the day of the week you want it to post, give it a date, time, topic, which platforms this post is for if you want to use photo or video for the post, your CTA, headline, the body content, and any hashtags if you are publishing to a social media platform like Twitter or Instagram.

Day _____ Date _____

Time _____ Topic _____

Platform

Photo & Video _____

Call-to-action _____

Headline _____

Content _____

_____

_____

_____

_____

_____

Hashtags _____

_____

_____

⬇ Download a copy of this worksheet at UnifyYourMarketing.com

Content Calendar

Date	Platform	Topic	Photo or Video	CTA Link	Headline	Content	Link	Hashtags

Use software to save your sanity

Use a social media manager or scheduling apps to plan out posts in advance. These will automatically post for you on the date and time you decide so you don't have to think twice about it later.

Apps like Hootsuite, Buffer, Later, HeroPost, etc are just some of the social media apps you can use to get your content out there.

Batching your content creation

Batch your content creation to be the most effective and do some deep work rather than a bit here and a bit there.

"Batching" means to block out a big chunk of time to create more than one piece of content for the upcoming schedule.

Generally speaking, the more focused you can be when creating content as a whole, distraction-free, the better the outcome.

For the Bear Wade brand, we block out one session that is about an hour-long each week to write out my filming outline and about 2 hours the following day to film and transfer footage to my editor.

I can generally shoot one episode in one filming session, but that episode gets broken up into 4 or 5 segments that are shared on social media.

This is great for publishing content consistently, allowing for maximum exposure with an episode out once every two weeks and social media clips out three times a week. Don't beat yourself up if you fall off track. Just get back to it when you can and keep on creating.

If you start to get stressed about your current content output schedule, it could be time to re-evaluate how often you post. You don't want to risk burning out.

If you don't have enough content straight from your video content, use images to fill in the gaps. Consistency + value = profits

The same goes for publishing. Schedule a few weeks of social media posts, email campaigns, and videos to be premiered on YouTube, then you don't have to be clicking a button at 7am on a Saturday because that is when you have found it is the best time to release a video on YouTube for your type of content.

Man, it feels so good to be on top of things! With a good amount of content ideas generated you can easily schedule things out a week or two and be on the proverbial beach sippin' margs while you continue to reach your audience and bring in more sales! ~Cheers!~ #workgoals

CHAPTER 11

KEY TAKEAWAYS

The value of consistency

· Value is more important than frequency
· Batch your content creation

CHAPTER 12

TEAM ROLES

Distribute the responsibilities.

CONSIDER HIRING A CONTRACTOR

It can be exhausting to be at the beginning of the pipeline and the end, because you will get overwhelmed with production analysis paralysis. To avoid this and maintain a sustainable pipeline, delegate roles to the right talent on your team. The key to delivering inspiring content on a consistent basis, is to find someone to help you.

Not only will this be more efficient and streamlined, but also it will ensure content doesn't fall through the cracks and reaches your audience on all of your communication channels.

Three Publishing Personalities

I think there are three personalities that you need on your publication team to be successful. Looking at the personality types of your current team, who is a content creator, who is naturally an editor, and who is a content publisher?

Content creators

Writers, videographers, photographers, storyboard experts.

Content creators are great at starting something and getting it off the ground. They see the whole picture and can see how to bring this element into this story and that person who would be great to bring into this content creation process and bring it to life.

If you don't have this personality in leadership, find a creative person who can get content ideas out of leadership and run with it. Your team leaders can always be part of the editing process. It is easier to edit something rather than to start something totally new.

Editors

Editors are the type of people that are great at seeing a current problem and adjusting it for the better.

Sometimes they might not be good at starting projects but can pick them up once they are roughed in and get them polished up and to the next level before publishing.

They are good at restructuring or rewording concepts, and are typically great with language and copy proofing, i.e. knowing grammar rules, punctuation, and can spellcheck for you.

They can also give the creators perspective on if this is too much industry/insider language, or need more explanation, or if you need examples or illustrations in certain spots of your content.

Having good content editors can bring fresh eyes, perspective, and clarity to what you create.

Publishers

You are going to need tech-savvy AND consistent personalities to be your content publishers. I think a consistent personality is more important, because you can teach them the software, but not make someone consistent as easily.

You can't do this alone

If you are a one-person operation, I'm here to tell you; you can't do it all. You can't afford to not publish and get your brand script out there. That's the whole point of this book, remember?

When you first start, look for a reasonably priced intern at your local college. Or, set aside a small portion of your monthly budget to hire someone who is passionate about sharing your story and brand with the public.

There are other places like UpWork.com, Freelance.com, and Fivver.com where you can find skilled help. Just make sure you interview and vet each person before hiring anyone. We'll talk more about this in the next chapter. Here's how this impacted Red Meat Lover.

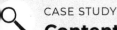

Content Production Pipelines

Company: Red Meat Lover

Industry: YouTube and cooking blog

Size: 2 employees and 5 contractors

Goal: Increase content creation from 1x/month to 1x/week.

Challenge: Content production was slow and clunky.

YouTube show Red Meat Lover has gained a great following over the past few years. Originally most of the responsibility was split between two people, but as the audience and team grew, it was way too much to do, and lots of tasks were dropped.

The ideal schedule was to release a video every week, which was not only way more work but lots more variables to manage. It was imperative to implement a project management system to track the video production progress as well as a content production pipeline.

Our original content production pipeline for RML:

Pre-production

- Joe: Research recipes, talk to the butcher, craft recipe, pack cooking gear, grocery shop; bring to filming
- Bear: Responsible for all gear tasks; bring to filming

Shoot day

- Joe, film 4-6 video recipes in one full day.
- Bear: Sets up the cameras, lights, mics, and narrates the first recipe to film.
- Assistant: Setup gear, help with filming, and help Joe with cleaning dishes

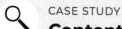
Content Production Pipelines

Post-production

- Bear: Transfer footage to external hard drive
- Bear: Sort footage and images
- Bear: Back up first hard drive
- Editor: Edit first video
- Joe: reviews draft
- Editor: Updates edit and uploads to YouTube
- Editor: Create a thumbnail

Delivery

- Joe: works on the best title, keywords, and tags
- Joe: Schedule video release
- Renee: Post recipe on our website
- Ty: Post video on social media
- Renee: Email the video to our database of followers
- Rinse. Repeat.

We assign tasks to each individual on our team and they move it along in Trello when they are finished with their part of the project. The content production pipeline evolves, as new team members have brought unique skills and it's really cool to see the way our team work develops organically.

 Pro Tip

Use software whenever you can to help automate your systems, it's a game-changer. We currently use Trello, which is pretty simple to use, to give each video recipe an identity and track its process from ideation to filming, editing to sharing.

Content Pipeline

PRE-PRODUCTION

Team Member   Task

PRODUCTION

Team Member   Task

POST-PRODUCTION

Team Member   Task

DELIVERY

Team Member   Task

CHAPTER 12

KEY TAKEAWAYS

Distribute the responsibilities

- Content creators
- Editors
- Publishers

DO YOU FEEL LIKE A ROCKSTAR YET?

You friggin' should! You're crushing it now with a plan to produce consistent, engaging, and helpful content across all of your channels, with defined roles to manage your content calendar of layout topics, production schedules, and assets.

Don't forget, the goal is to create content once and run it through your pipeline to make the most of your time and effort. You have so much value to add to your community, don't stop now!

Only one last step, Step 5: Scaling, to go before you're swimming in a vault of gold coins Scrooge McDuck style. Ha!

UNIFY STEP 5

SCALING

Track and analyze your data, order fulfillment, and scale your team so you can grow your company beyond your time and effort.

01
DEFINING

02
BUILDING

03
GROWING

04
ONGOING

05
SCALING

CHAPTER 13

ANALYZE WHAT IS WORKING

If you take the time to measure your data and processes, you have the ability to improve them.

We want to focus on the WHO, not the HOW when scaling a business.

It's time to scale what you've built and watch profits soar! This is when we take it from a business and turn it into an empire! (As we pet a white kitten in our lap and smoke a long monochrome Cruella stick.) Let's tackle this by breaking it all down into bite-sized pieces.

- Analyze what's working, and adjust or cut what isn't.
- Fine-tune your project management system so you can track and fulfill orders.
- Create standard operating procedures (SOPs) to track progress
- Schedule ongoing reviews to maintain your scaling process.

Let's do this!!!

With the groundwork you have done in Steps 1-4 you may already be bringing in more sales and fulfilling more orders. That is huge! You're feeling confident and motivated by the momentum to scale your business.

But what if I'm not growing my sales yet?

If you aren't bringing in more sales just yet, don't panic! This book is your blueprint and you can always go back to any step to refine it. Don't scale what isn't working, instead, take a second and pause here. Take a step back and review all the work you've put in starting with your brand steps. See if you can diagnose what is preventing your business from getting off the ground. Trying to grow with a ton of problem areas will make you go crazy! (speaking from experience) Remember, work to hone what is working before you scale it.

Nerds, unite!

Dust off that pocket protector and fire up those spreadsheets! It is time to analyze your efforts and outcomes. This is also a pivotal moment to take a pause and closely examine your efforts. Business is a grand experiment, and it's necessary to scrutinize what is driving your ROI and what is potentially holding you back.

> *"What gets measured gets improved."*
>
> PETER DRUCKER

KPIs

Oh god, here we go with more acronyms! This one is handy, so grab a pen and paper or your favorite spreadsheet software.

Key performance indicators (KPIs) are marketing buzzwords for sure and one of the least understood terms in business development. They have an ambiguous meaning that can include any advertising metric or data used to measure performance, making them more difficult than they need be for businesses looking to grow their customer base.

For me, the whole goal of defining your KPIs is to have a common trackable metric and figuring out how to optimize it so that we can make more money!

Here are some examples of some general KPIs:

- Shorten the sales cycle by half
- Generate 50% more leads
- Create a new usage occasion
- Get loyal customers to buy 30% or more

So, what are some of your key metrics that you can identify in your business that once you see them improve it will reflect that your business is getting healthier? Dude, seriously, stop reading, and jot down a few ideas!

It's Time to Track. Compare. Repeat.

In my best McConaughey, "Well, Alright, Alright, Alright." as I pull a long strand of hay from out of the corner of my mouth. "Now we are getting down to where the rubber meets the road." (You could hear the subtle whistle in my voice too, couldn't you?!) It is time to face the light and see how all of our work has been performing in the market. It's time to Track. Compare. And Repeat.

Track

Marketing is a complex process, but it all boils down to one question: what are the drivers behind your success? Marketing encompasses so many elements that you'll want to track -- campaigns, emails, social media posts and ads. However, if things aren't going as planned with sales or costs starting to pile up on balance sheets then something needs attention. The first thing I would do after identifying an issue in my marketing efforts was ask myself "What caused this?"

Compare

What was the cost-to-profit ratio of that campaign? Sure you might have sold 100 more units and made $20,000 but how much did it cost to make those sales? Was it worth an additional $25,000 on top of your initial investment just so you can sell a hundred extra pieces.

This may seem like a good idea at first glance because the additional revenue would outweigh any losses by quite a bit. However this is not always true as well-intentioned campaigns often end up costing their owners money instead through wasted time or investments in marketing efforts which do not produce results.

Analysis paralysis

If God has granted me one superpower, it is the gift of overthinking data to the point of being incapacitated. My mom and dad are so proud of their little Bear! But here is my advice. Working with a team. If you can surround yourself with other nerds who love to crunch data, it can be REALLY fun to try and learn more through your numbers.

Try and gamify your data

Don't burn yourself out by capturing ALL of the data, or being too granular. Stick to the macro as a business owner and see the big picture of what is working and what isn't. Make it fun! Respect the data! (I feel like I should print T-shirts with that on it.)

As you close out your data analysis session consider: What exciting things can I do next to bring value to my audience?

Repeat

This is why it's important to create a routine that will help you be more disciplined. If you block out time every month, quarter or year on your calendar for analyzing the results of what works and learning from

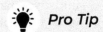 *Pro Tip*

I've said it once, I'll say it again! What gets scheduled gets done - make sure you schedule in a monthly analysis, quarterly analysis and annual analysis or else you will find it incredibly hard to stop and make it happen on a whim. As a business owner you have plenty on your plate! Make time to make analysis happen and you won't regret it.

mistakes then this can give you confidence in how well your plan has been working - no excuses!

After you analyze individually on a macro level, take time to work with your team to analyze together on a more micro level. This allows you and your team to stay in sync and unified in your ongoing efforts.

Make a list of your successes

Make a list with your team to celebrate what campaigns, ads, and marketing initiatives made a splash (and a profit). After you've made your list, do an in-depth analysis to figure out what worked within the initiative and why. Next are just a few examples of questions to get you started.

Biggest successes

- Did you have great visuals that caught people's attention?
- Was it good timing due to seasonality in your field?
- Was the call-to-action easy to convert a sale?
- Was it your irresistible offer?
- Was it from one big order or many small orders?
- How many new customers did you acquire vs. previous customers?
- How are you stewarding new customer relationships?
- How can we reproduce this campaign with repeated results?
- What was the overall ROI (in percentage form) of the campaign?

Scrutinize what went wrong

What were the biggest busts of your marketing efforts? Don't dwell on who is to blame or beat yourself up for something that didn't work, but you should DEFINITELY take a moment and label what didn't work and possible causes to try and mitigate them in the future! You know what they say about the definition of insanity - you can't keep doing the same thing over and over and expect a different outcome. Try to not get bogged down by the "down" side to your campaign, use it as a springboard for new amazing ideas.

Why didn't your campaign succeed?

- Were your creative assets not eye-catching enough?
  - (Messaging, photography, video, graphic design)
- Bad timing in the market?

- Poor call-to-action? How would I know it is a bad CTA?
- Poor ad spend?
- Not a good enough offer?
- Just not the right solution for your market's problem?

Feeling a bit like a human punching bag after that exercise? Take a breather, take a walk, do a little yoga. Realize that anything you've analyzed and realized isn't working isn't a reflection on you doing a terrible job, in fact, your analysis proves your aptitude and energy to do things "right".

Define your action plan moving forward

Take a moment with your team and end on a high note. Circle back around and name a few things that you want to do coming up in the future that you know worked. Get your energy back up, focus on some of the Key Performance Indicators (KPIs) that were successes and align with your team to get ready to take what you've all learned and evolve it into the next iteration of your marketing strategy. You got this!

CHAPTER 13

KEY TAKEAWAYS

Scaling

- What gets measured gets improved
- List your successes
- Scrutinize what went wrong
- Define your action plan moving forward

CHAPTER 14

ORDER FULFILLMENT

Sales are worth nothing if you can't fulfill your orders.

 CONSIDER HIRING A CONTRACTOR

3% of customers say they won't shop with a retailer again for at least a month after a negative delivery experience. Another 38% of customers say they won't shop with retailers again at all. Because of this, it is imperative that your customer service constantly remains one of our top priorities. From communicating how easy it is to navigate your site and handling complaints, you need to have processes in place to be able to appropriately handle customers with excellence and ease from start to finish.

One element that can influence the way customers think about your company once they have purchased from you, is how effectively you can deliver that order, and to what degree can you exceed their expectations. If you over-promise and under-deliver, you will not only cost yourself and your company time and money but you will upset the customer and lose business as well. An upset customer is also likely to leave a negative review, which could change future business.

What people think and feel about your company is branding.

Some scenarios you might be familiar with:

Imagine having a leaky faucet. The water is actively running and you can't turn the handle far enough to get it to shut off. What do you do?

First, reach out to your device. Then, you remember seeing a nice truck at the stoplight next to you just a few days ago with the words "We stop leaky faucets" scrawled across its side. Do you remember the name? You can look them up and go to their website. It looks great and you can sign-up for an appointment for tomorrow morning. Great! You put a bucket under the faucet and move on, happy to make an appointment. If you feel empowered to have a resolution!

Morning rolls around. You've been able to replace buckets this morning and haven't lost too much water overall. You did spill a bit on the floor and got your socks wet. Ugh.

You anticipate the plumber showing up any minute now per the confirmation email.

But nobody shows up.

You wait an hour and finally call the number at the bottom of their email and website.

"I'm sorry, Ma'am, I do see your name on the calendar, but we don't have enough technicians working today. Can we schedule for later this week?"

Insert your favorite cuss words here.

It doesn't matter how good your marketing is if you can't fulfill the orders.

Trust is broken, and you both lose.

When it comes to tracking systems, the cleaner the better

Whatever tracking system software you use, it needs to be easy to use and available to all team members anytime and anywhere. As mentioned in the previous chapter, I personally love to use and recommend Trello. It's free for basic users and has incredible workflow processes that make things easy to delegate and track all in one convenient location. All someone needs to sign up is an email address and internet connection. You can work with teams the world over in one location with ease.

Like I said at the beginning of this book, there is no amount of marketing you can do if you can't fulfill your orders quickly while maintaining quality.

Grimco Marketing Department

Company: Grimco Marketing Department

Industry: Manufacturing

Company Size: 1,000

Goal: Tracking system

Challenge: Grimco is a sign manufacturing company with branches all over North America. For a time, I worked as their part-time Chief Marketing Officer to unify their marketing plan and their marketing department. The goal was to get everyone in their marketing department using the same systems, as well as all of the people they serve, both internally and externally, onto one system, so they could track and fulfill requests efficiently.

The challenges included:

- Design requests were received from lots of different departments
- There was no priority system based on the project description
- Everything was labeled as "due ASAP"
- The lack of system led to team burnout and resentment

Marketing and design requests came not just from all eight product division managers, corporate leadership, sales managers, their website developers, vendors, as well as their own digital marketing team, all of which we are going to refer to as "clients" in this story.

Mo, the newly promoted head of the marketing department, was a great leader and expert digital marketer. He struggled to establish authority and buy-in from the rest of the team. He hired a consultant to break the tension and empower his team to do things differently.

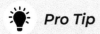 **Pro Tip**

Remember this tactic of bringing in reinforcements whenever you attempt to revamp a department with a new team lead.

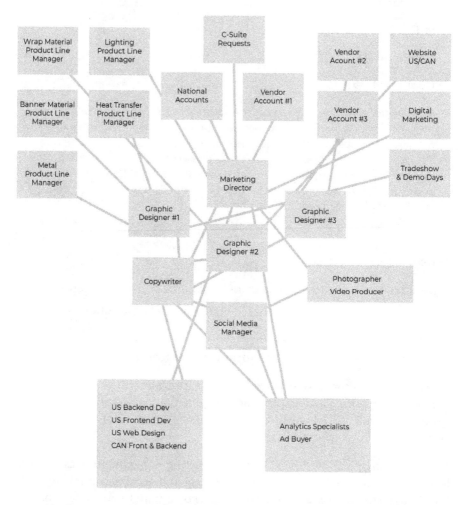

You'll see that after mapping out how the department worked there was too much time communicating to one person at a time rather than the right person at the right time.

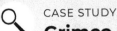
Step 1: Team survey

I started by conducting surveys with each team member.

The goal:

- Learn the details of the team role
- Determine what needs to change for their role
- Identify their goals and hopes for the future with their career

This gives you insight into their motivation and can help you gauge their interest and longevity with your company so you know if they are worth the investment of onboarding, if they are strictly a "one and done" freelancer.

Step 2: Map the workflow

We tracked and mapped out order requests, and developed a system to fulfill order requests through their Project Management Software. We were able to map out the system visually for all team members to easily understand.

This visualization helped the president see exactly what his teams were facing on a daily basis and hone in on what was most important for the business to focus on. He knew his teams were overextended and couldn't figure out if he needed to scale his team or develop a more efficient workflow. From there, the importance of implementing a system to fulfill design requests became glaringly obvious.

Step 3: Define what is valuable work

Upon receiving the request, Mo will determine whether the request is profitable enough for the business to dedicate resources to it. This meant he would either:

1. To fulfill that request.
2. Go back to the project requestee and clarify the need, or refer them to another solution.

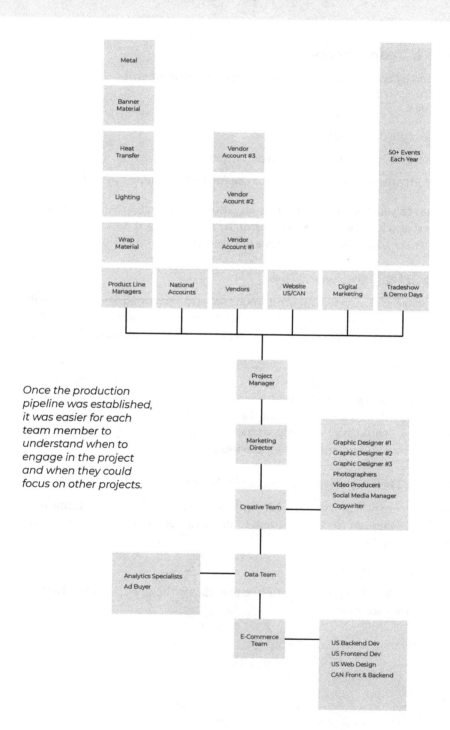

Metal

Banner Material

Heat Transfer

Lighting

Wrap Material

Vendor Account #3

Vendor Account #2

Vendor Account #1

50+ Events Each Year

Product Line Managers | National Accounts | Vendors | Website US/CAN | Digital Marketing | Tradeshow & Demo Days

Project Manager

Marketing Director

Once the production pipeline was established, it was easier for each team member to understand when to engage in the project and when they could focus on other projects.

Creative Team

Graphic Designer #1
Graphic Designer #2
Graphic Designer #3
Photographers
Video Producers
Social Media Manager
Copywriter

Analytics Specialists
Ad Buyer

Data Team

E-Commerce Team

US Backend Dev
US Frontend Dev
US Web Design
CAN Front & Backend

Step 4: Give each project a tracking number

Upon approval, each project was given a tracking number to give each request an identity moving forward. This allowed team members to save time by not having to track down where a project was in the process, ensured projects would not fall off the radar and also helped the team better understand their value within the production process. The marketing team began thinking of themselves as a production and publishing team because of the new systems in place ala Henry Ford's assembly line.

Step 5: Assign the project to a team member

After being given a tracking number, each project was assigned to a project manager, who was charged with managing the customer relationship and pushing it through the production pipeline. The PM assigned the project to the Creative Director, who would talk with the creative team about the project or if it was a small request just go straight to the creative, (graphic designer, photographer, etc).

Once the project designs were created, an internal review process would take place to get another set of eyes to review for quality before sending it to the "client."

Once it is approved by the client, a website page will be built out, along with campaign materials for the digital marketing team to schedule via email and social media with the project manager overseeing all steps throughout.

Step 6: Track the process and make adjustments

I ran a series of follow-up one-on-one meetings to check the status of this new system. As a result of the new production pipeline and clarity in the team's process I was thrilled to find out stress, and inner-team tension was greatly reduced over time. Furthermore, their effectiveness in fulfilling requests maintained high quality, consistently creating positive interactions with their clients and repeat business. ***Cowabunga!***

Your Fulfillment Process

Your fulfillment process will take a bit of work to determine, but the more automated it can be, the better your chances of growing your profits and reducing errors on a continual basis.

Here is an example of what your process could look like:

- *Order received through your website (channel)*
- *New card created in project management software*
  - *Using the name & main contact, address, phone, email, products ordered, additional details and transaction number.*
- *Contact info is added to CRM / order is assigned to a Project Manager*
- *Order approved by leadership*
- *Order assigned to project manager to determine which team will fulfill the request*
- *Project Manager (PM) moves the project to a team specialist to fulfill*
- *Order is shipped by team specialist*
- *PM sends confirmation email*
- *PM follow up*
- *The onboarding drip sequence is deployed*

While this is very common sense stuff here, it will make a world of difference in your team's productivity and feeling of accomplishment if you can clearly define it and communicate that process to your team.

You will most likely have other steps in your process that make your company, products, and services unique, so embrace those and make them fit your needs! Most important is that you're continuing to deliver valuable service to your clients on a timely basis while putting effort into stewarding current and new customer relationships.

"Building a good customer experience does not happen by accident, it happens by design."

CLARE MUSCUTT

CHAPTER 14

KEY TAKEAWAYS

Order fulfillment

- The cleaner the tracking, the better
- Case study: Grimco
  - Team survey
  - Map the workflow
  - Give each project a tracking number
  - Assign the project to a team member
  - Track progress and make adjustments
- Define your fulfillment process

CHAPTER 15

SCALE YOUR TEAM AND DELEGATE

Reclaim your time and do the work that is most valuable to growing the company.

CONSIDER HIRING A CONTRACTOR

How much time are you wasting per week?

A study from Inc.com found that we are losing an average of 21.8 hours per week because of handling low-value emails, constant interruptions throughout the workday, and putting out preventable fires, oh, and the non-productive meetings! AHHHH!

We need to reclaim our time and do the work that is most valuable to growing the company. We don't want the CEO out shoveling the parking lot. Sure they can do it, but is that what is best for the company? Finding the right teammates is essential to an organization's health.

Know when it's time to hire

So, how do you know when you are ready to hire? Well, the short answer is, if you have started making money, you are ready. But, really, it comes down to that balance of: "can you afford to do it?" versus "can you afford not to do it?"

You can hire too quickly and deplete your savings quickly. If you wait too long, you can get bogged down and not be able to fulfill orders quick enough which doesn't work either. When you get to the point where your business and orders outweigh your time (also taking into account the fact you are doing so much other stuff in the business like content creation) you need to consider delegating. You may be afraid to entrust tasks to new people and I get it, but every successful business has a team behind it.

Working alone is very hard, so finding one part-time contractor can go a long way to scale your business, keep your overhead low, and your to-do list short.

Define your top five tasks

Begin by jotting down your top five tasks that you perform on any given day/week/month.

Let's say it is:

1. Answering email

2. Reading mail and paying bills

3. Managing your team

4. Working with your vendors

5. Sales phone calls

Which of these items can only YOU specifically do? Go ahead and pick apart each item and figure out how to do them smarter, faster, or not at all. And by that I mean, delegate or cut out of your role.

1. Answering email

- Different types of emails you're receiving and responding to.
- Could this job be done by someone else? Or even just parts of this job?

2. Reading mail and paying bills

- How much mail is coming in?
- How many tasks are generated by incoming mail?
- Could this job be done by someone else?

3. Managing your team

- How much time do you spend managing your team?
- Are there ways you could improve efficiency? For example, instead of fielding 5, 10-minute meetings a week based on specific situations, schedule time on a recurring basis and touch base with each team member to answer any questions or concerns. This is also a great way to keep an eye on what your team is doing without micromanaging.
- Could someone else do this job? Probably not, but adding a project manager or other management role might help you save time!

4. Working with your vendors

- How often do you spend time working with vendors?
- How many tasks are you managing after each vendor call?
- Could you hire help to manage vendor relations and project management?

5. Sales phone calls

- How many calls do you take each week?
- Is there a way to have different team members field different topics?

The answers to each of these questions will differ depending on your business and preferences. Take the time to look in depth at your daily tasks and ensure that the work you are doing fits into what you are best at and also love to do. This will keep you motivated when life as a business owner gets tough.

What Can You Delegate?

So, what are the tasks that you can delegate to team members or contractors that don't need your direct attention and still move forward with your guidance? Is it Bookkeeping? Maybe hiring a project manager would help? Maybe hiring an administrative assistant to answer calls and emails, based upon your guidance, would cut down on time. You may love social media but you hate sales.

Focus more on what you're good at and less on spreading yourself thin with tasks that you don't enjoy or that you know could be done better by someone else. Hire someone trained in sales psychology to do this for you. Give them a Calendly with a schedule and route all your prospective clients to them. For each sale they close, offer them a slice of the commission. Now you've got a business system in place that may increase your profits and decrease your stress.

Hate social media? Hire a social media manager. This person can spend all the time you don't have researching trends, hashtags, coming up with ideas, and posting for you. If you don't like the time it takes to edit, create your content and then outsource it to an editor to chop up into YouTube and TikTok videos. There is someone out there for everything. A good business leader can recognize their strengths as well as their weaknesses and know when and where to delegate tasks that could be done better and quicker by someone else.

Administrative work

What if taking too much of your time is reading mail and paying bills? Having an assistant could help move these tasks along. You could still sign the checks giving you some control, with less busy work.

Virtual Assistants are a wonderful tool to have today and you can hire them on an as-needed basis from anywhere in the world. Even better? VAs are often niched down, like any other profession. Need someone who can help edit photos? Find that VA. Need a VA who is also a social media manager? They're out there. Know what you need, and look for it from the start to ensure success.

Sales associate

Or hiring a director of sales, or sales associate could help get those cold calls off of your plate, and, with proper training, could start to deliver warmer leads for you to close. Or as mentioned above, they can close it for you.

Recognize your strengths and if this is not one of them hire someone who is better at it so you can close more sales.

Social media manager

With this role outsourced, you can still be the one to make the content, but leave it to someone else who can manage the postings, comments, hashtags, and that will break you away from all of the time and attention social media can suck out of your day.

✏ EXERCISE   WHAT CAN YOU DELEGATE?

What are the top five tasks that you'd like to take off of your plate and start to delegate?

1. _____

2. _____

3. _____

4. _____

5. _____

How to hand over tasks with less anxiety

Delegating your tasks to others can be a hard thing to do. I have a saying that you can use to help hand over your process to a team member with ease for both you and them. After some time you will establish trust, accountability and responsibility within your team and be able to hand off tasks more easily knowing they will get done on time and to your standards.

Go write this on your dry erase board:

- I do, you watch.
- I do, you help.
- You do, I help.
- You do, I watch.

This is a way to slowly handover a task or role to someone else without overwhelming them, and giving you the chance to communicate your beliefs and strategies to that with which you want to hand over.

I'm going to use making a peanut butter and jelly sandwich as my teaching example here, just so we are all on the same page.

So first, I'm going to do the task, and they are going to watch me do it, while I explain my process to them, just talking out loud in real time. Because I'm showing and telling, we are quicker to retain this information.

Example: First I'll grab my ingredients of peanut butter, jelly, bread, a plate and butter knife. Then, I'll open the peanut butter, dip the knife in the peanut butter jar to grab a glob, and spread peanut butter over the bread. Then, I'll wipe the knife on the other piece of bread to clean the knife off before grabbing a glob of jelly from the container and smearing it over that piece of bread. (I don't want peanut butter getting in the jelly jar.) I then put the two pieces of bread together, marrying the peanut butter and the jelly into one. Angels Rejoice! I then cut the sandwich into two triangles, because everyone knows it tastes better that way.

Next, I'll do the task again, but with their help on parts of it, which will engage a bit of their brain in a different way, and they will have the opportunity to ask clarifying questions.

Example: I'll talk them through it, but have them "control" the knife. And if I have any tips, I might take the knife back and show them my technique for spreading the peanut butter, let's say, without tearing the bread.

After that, they take the lead, and start the task, where they do the talking and even "run the knife" which I assist.

Example: They do the majority of the work, but I'll help out getting the next ingredient for them, to speed up the process and get their muscle memory more in tune.

Lastly, I'll have them do it one more time from start to finish without any help or instruction. If they can do that, I have a lot more confidence in handing that task over, and they now have the ability to be more valuable to the company, WHILE saving you precious time!

> *Example: They make the last sandwich all on their own! Now we have four sandwiches! Yippee!!*

If you can show them a process that has been successful, and slowly let it go so they can take it over, you both win!

Don't skip a step here. Be deliberate. What seems as easy as making a PB&J to you might be really new to someone else, so respect them and allow for each step to unfold. Don't micromanage. Allow them to start thinking beyond your process and nurture it. You don't really want to have a clone of yourself, but someone who can have the time and talent outside of you to enhance your steps.

You will be able to provide better customer service and your customers will thank you.

After a while, you can follow up with them and double-check that they are representing your work. And if you hired the right person, they might even enhance your process, or come up with a more effective way that you hadn't even considered.

Create standard operating procedures (SOPs)

For every role that you want to delegate to another team member, create an SOP or standard operating procedure. This easily tracks your process and communicates it to the person who is going to take over that role.

Even better, have them take notes while you are showing them their task, and you can clean it up a bit at the end. After your teammate has been working on that task for a while, ask them to update it every 6-12 months. You can have it be part of their annual review process if you want.

These are SO helpful to have because, as your team moves on to other roles within your company or to of your next endeavor outside your company, you have a quick way to onboard the next person, without having to refigure it out.

After a while you will have stepped away from the day-to-day "button clicking", so tracking their process will be essential to getting back up and running.

If I'm working with a team member virtually, or want to have a resource that I can share with multiple people or have something they can reference often, then I'll screen record myself doing the task on my computer. There are a handful of screen recorders out there, but the one I'm currently using is called Loom. (Loom.com)

If you are doing a job that isn't on your computer then I recommend at least recording the SOP on video with your phone, and then you can also have written SOP to accompany it.

We use SOPs like a checklist of tasks that need to be completed in order to achieve the desired outcome.

Here is an example of an SOP in our company:

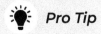 *Pro Tip*

I use screen recordings of me doing this and will sometimes include screenshots of each step as part of the SOP so they know what to look for. This can also be done by screen sharing on a live video chat.

Here is an example of an SOP in our company:

WEBSITE CONTENT PRODUCER SOP

Initial steps
- *Log into our website*
- *Log into Trello*
- *Log into YouTube*
- *Log into Rev.com*
- *Get the YouTube video link from Trello*
- *Make sure it is set to "Private" on YouTube*

At Rev.com
- *Go to Rev.com and, in the upper right-hand corner, click the button that says "New Order."*
- *Create a new order on Rev.com for an "Automated Transcription"*
- *Follow the prompts to complete the purchase using the card on file.*

- *Once you have finished your order, go to "My Orders" to wait for the transcription to finish.*
- *It can take anywhere from 3-20 minutes to complete.*
- *Refresh your browser to see the status change from "In process" to "Complete"*
- *Once it is complete, click the download button and download it as an .Docx file with timecodes included checkbox checked.*
- *Next, upload the transcription .docx file to the corresponding Trello card, so we have it for the future.*

On our website

- *Next, go to the website and in the dashboard, create a new post, by clicking on the "Post" button on the navigation bar on the left side of the screen.*
- *The next title is the post with the name taken from the transcription document, which should be the same name taken from YouTube.*
- *Then, add a featured image located in the bottom right corner of the post page.*
- *Also, in that same column, there is a tags and categories section. Please check the boxes applicable as well as add tags that you find suitable for this particular post.*

On our YouTube channel

- *Next, go to our YouTube page, and grab the embed code, by going to the video page, and click on the "Share" button below the video window.*
- *Click on "Embed" and copy that embed code and paste it into the website's post body section.*

Now back to our website

- *The body section is the main section where you would write a copy.*
- *You'll notice that the video pops up in the edit window if you pasted it correctly.*
- *Next, open the transcription document, and cut and paste that entire document into the body of the post, below the video.*
- *Next, skim the document and make any adjustments to the transcription as you see fit.*

- *Please add section headings and add H1 tags and H2 tags as you see fit throughout.*
- *Also, add any inbound and outbound links as you see fit.*
- *Next, go to the Trello card and download any attached images that you see working well for the post and add them into the post throughout.*
- *Add alt tags to each image describing what is in each image.*
- *Once done, set a publishing date and time and save the document.*
- *After that, go down to the Yoast plugin and build out the meta description, keywords, etc. You can review the Yoast plugin SOP for more details.*
- *Next, save your document.*

In Trello

- *Move the Trello card to the next task in line.*
- *Thanks so much for your hard work to grow this company!*

The Hiring Process

If you are looking to hire some outside help, I'd start with hiring part-time freelancers who work on an as-needed basis. They will bring the specialized skills you need to the team. You won't have to set up infrastructure, like payroll, benefits packages, and their own place to work. Freelancers or contract workers usually work remotely.

The best place to start is by creating a job post that you can add to your website under your "Work with Us" page. You can also use websites like Upwork, Freelancer, or Indeed. You can even jump on Facebook and search groups for what it is you're hiring. Many groups will allow you to post that you are looking for work. This is a great way to connect and get some resumes as well!

Over the past few decades, I have created forms to post a job, take applicants, and a checklist to ensure the onboarding process goes smoothly.

If you use these forms, you can save a ton of time tracking down this information as you go, and it creates four checkpoints when hiring someone. If you don't use these forms, you can get bogged down with collecting information you need for taxes, security, and getting them onboarded quickly and efficiently.

Here are the four checkpoints to working with another person:

- Job posting
- Job application
- New contractor information
- New hire onboarding checklist

Here is an example of one of our job postings for a Project Manager:

Project Manager

Our close-knit company is looking for a self-motivated individual who is willing to go the extra mile; someone with amazing communication skills and the ability to write and verbally communicate with clients and contractors. Comfortable working in a virtual environment while moving projects through our production pipeline.

Primary responsibilities include, but are not limited to:

- *Manage production timelines*
- *Ability to be on Zoom calls with customers, and cheer them on and support them in the production process.*
- *Ability to move projects through the production pipeline and hold teams accountable*
- *Provide support to leadership and creative teams*

Minimum Qualifications:

- *College graduate (preferred)*
- *Have a functioning computer, internet connection, and phone*

Preferred Qualifications:

- *Marketing, Communications or English degree*
- *Independent self-starter, detail-oriented and efficient time management*
- *Exemplify a strong work ethic and operate with the highest level of integrity*
- *Strong communication and written skills*

Part-time position opening. X-X hours per week. Starting at $X/per hour, but dependent on experience.

This is a 1099 contractor position.

Then we'll direct them to our website to apply which will have this form for them to fill out:

Contractor Application

Personal

Name (First, Last) _____

Permanent address*

   Street address _____

   Address Line 2 _____

   City _____

   State _____

   ZIP code _____

Phone number* _____

Email* _____

Website _____

Have you ever applied to this organization before?* ☐ Yes ☐ No

Have you been employed by this organization before?* ☐ Yes ☐ No

Employment Interests

Which position are you applying for?* _____

Skills & Abilities

What programs and apps do you use and what level of competence from 1 - 10 would you rate yourself? _____

_____

_____

Availability

Date available to start* _____

Type of employment you are seeking* ☐ Part-time ☐ Full-Time

Availability* (days and times) _____

How were you referred to our organization?*

☐ Advertisement   ☐ Colleague   ☐ Friend

Education/U.S. Military Service

Where did you attend high school & college?*

School name and address _____

Major_____

Years completed _____

GPA_____

Degree/Diploma_____

Are you taking any educational course(s) presently?*

☐ Yes   ☐ No   ☐ I will be soon

Have you ever served in the U.S. Armed Services?   ☐ Yes ☐ No

---

Acknowledgment

Digital Signature (printing your first name + middle initial + last name will act as your digital signature.) _____

Date _____

Resume upload (optional)

Would you like to add a cover letter?   ☐ Yes ☐ No

⬇ Download a copy of this resource at UnifyYourMarketing.com

Review applications

The next step is to review their resumes and applications, find your top 3-5 candidates, and set up interviews. I separated my applications into two piles. Nos and maybes for the first round. Then, of the Maybes, I'll find the top 3-5 for interviews. These are all based upon a curve of who applies, so pick your favorite candidate based on the application/resume, but don't rank them in stone until after you conduct an interview to know more about them.

Interview questions

I'll be honest with you. I don't really have interview questions that I work from, but I do have a kickoff question and a closing statement that facilitates interviews well. Because I'm a person that thinks of himself as intuitive, I like to conduct my interviews either in person or over video. I try to stay away from email interviews or even phone interviews because I don't get enough non-verbal cues as I like to have when I interview someone in person.

Next, I have a list of questions that you can pick and choose from to get your interviews up and running.

Make sure you take care of them from here on out. "Did you find the place okay?" If not, remember that for the next person, you can offer a few tips to make finding the place easier. "Would you like some water?" The more you serve them, from this point on, the better the chance of them taking care of your company.

Start by telling them a bit about the business. Show them anything you can that helps them get a picture of what we do, the quality of work, and even meet some of the others in leadership.

After that, I turn it to them by saying, "So tell me a bit about you." Try and really get to know them. See what their underlying motivations are. If they talk about working with a team, and being creative, cool. If they ask questions about "how many hours can I get?" then you might have a problem. They are looking for a paycheck and it's not about generating results. Ask them about their career goals and see if that aligns with the job posting at all.

If you are hiring someone that is going to be a social media manager for you, but when you ask them about their goals, talking about traveling around the world as a dancer might not be the consistent personality you need in this role.

According to Society for Human Resource Management, it costs an average of $4,129 per hire and over 42 days to fill a position.

Now, I know that is for employees and not contractor labor, but even if it is half that, it is substantial money and effort to start to clone yourself.

You don't have to start with anyone but 5 hours a week will go really far in reclaiming your time and effort back to what your business needs most.

Some of the first rolls I replaced for me, were ones that took a lot of my time but didn't yield expert-needed results. Finding an admin assistant or virtual assistant is a great first hire. You can delegate tasks like travel, appointment settings, and email logistics to them, as well as posting them on your behalf to social media. They can also serve as your editor, as needed.

Interview questions examples

According to The Muse, here are 50 interview questions that you can use to learn more about your interviewee:

I'd only pick 5-10 of these questions, and I recommend that you know what questions you want to ask before the interview session.

- Tell me about yourself.
- How did you hear about this position?
- Why do you want to work at this company?
- Why do you want this job?
- Why should we hire you?
- What can you bring to the company?
- What are your greatest strengths?
- What do you consider to be your weaknesses?
- What is your greatest professional achievement?
- Tell me about a challenge you've faced at work, and how you dealt with it.
- Tell me about a time you demonstrated leadership skills.
- What's a time you disagreed with a decision that was made at work?
- Tell me about a time you made a mistake.
- Tell me about a time you failed.
- Why are you leaving your current job?
- Why were you fired?
- Why was there a gap in your employment?
- Can you explain why you changed career paths?

- What's your current salary?
- What do you like least about your job?
- What are you looking for in a new position?
- What type of work environment do you prefer?
- What's your work style?
- What's your management style?
- How would your boss and coworkers describe you?
- How do you deal with pressure or stressful situations?
- What do you like to do outside of work?
- Are you planning on having children?
- How do you prioritize your work?
- What are you passionate about?
- What motivates you?
- What are your pet peeves?
- How do you like to be managed?
- Do you consider yourself successful?
- Where do you see yourself in five years?
- How do you plan to achieve your career goals?
- What's your dream job?
- What other companies are you interviewing with?
- What makes you unique?
- What should I know that's not on your resume?
- What would your first 30, 60, or 90 days look like in this role?
- What are your salary expectations?
- What do you think we could do better of differently?
- When can you start?
- Are you willing to relocate?
- How many tennis balls can you fit into a limousine?
- If you were an animal, which one would you want to be?
- Sell me this pen.
- Is there anything else you'd like us to know?
- What questions do you have for me?

Hiring a new team member

Having cash flow to pay for this new hire is key to maintaining your investment. You should plan to have at least three months of savings allocated to pay that person if you were to run into an income dry spell.

If they have access to sensitive data or are customer-facing, and do more than just behind the scenes work for me, then I will next have them fill out a contractor information form, so if I ever need to track them down, (god help me) I can.

New Contractor Form

Personal

Name (First, Last) _____

Drivers license number*

Drivers license state*

Permanent address*

    Street address _____

    Address Line 2 _____

    City_____

    State_____

    ZIP code _____

Phone number* _____

Email*_____

Date of birth* _____

Social security number*

Do you have the legal right to live and work in the U.S.* ☐ Yes ☐ No

Have you applied to this organization before?*　　　☐ Yes ☐ No

Have you been employed by this organization before?* ☐ Yes ☐ No

Do you have any family, business, health, or social restrictions or obligations that would prevent you from performing the job responsibilities?*　　　☐ Yes ☐ No

Do you have any physical or mental condition or handicap which would endanger the health or safety of yourself and or others or that may affect your ability to perform the job(s) for which you are applying?* ☐ Yes ☐ No

Have you ever been convicted of a felony?* ☐ Yes ☐ No

Will you comply with the safety work and attendance policies of our organization? ☐ Yes ☐ No

Employment Interests

Which position are you applying for?* _____

Skills & Abilities

What programs and apps do you use and what level of competence from 1 - 10 would you rate yourself? _____

_____

Availability

Date available to start* _____

Type of employment you are seeking* ☐ Part-time ☐ Full-Time

Availability* (days and times) _____

How were you referred to our organization?*

☐ Advertisement ☐ Colleague ☐ Friend

Education/U.S. Military Service

Where did you attend high school & college?*

    School name and address _____

    Major _____

    Years completed _____

    GPA _____

    Degree/Diploma _____

Are you taking any educational course(s) presently?*

☐ Yes ☐ No ☐ I will be soon

Have you ever served in the U.S. Armed Services?   ☐ Yes ☐ No

References

List 3-5 people we may contact who are qualified to evaluate your capabilities. Do not include relatives. (Name , address, occupation, years known)

_____

_____

_____

_____

_____

_____

Employment History

Give employment records as complete as possible, listing current or most recent employers first. Show unemployment or self-employed periods and indicate dates and comment on each period. Include part-time or summer work.

Company name (most recent) _____

Address _____

Address Line 2 _____

City _____

State / Province / Region _____

ZIP / Postal code _____

Country _____

Phone _____

Dates employed _____

Job title _____

Base rate of pay (hour/week/month) _____

Description of duties _____

_____

_____

_____

Reason for leaving _____

May we contact this employer?   ☐ Yes ☐ No

Did you have another job before this one?   ☐ Yes ☐ No

I agree to a Drug Screening at the
company's expense.*   ☐ Yes ☐ No

I agree to a Criminal Background Check at the
company's expense.*   ☐ Yes ☐ No

Acknowledgment

Digital Signature (printing your first name + middle initial + last
name will act as your digital signature.) _____

Date _____

Resume upload (optional)

Would you like to add a cover letter?   ☐ Yes ☐ No

⬇ Download a copy of this resource at UnifyYourMarketing.com

And lastly, I use this checklist to get new team members onboarded and comfortable working within our ecosystem.

NEW HIRE ONBOARDING CHECKLIST

Two weeks prior to the start date

- [ ] Confirm start date & hourly rate
- [ ] Unify Creative Agency Contractor Information
- [ ] Employment Agreement
- [ ] Send new employee Unify's contact info
- [ ] Send W-4's federal & state
- [ ] Send W-9

One week prior to the start date

- [ ] Set-up applicable computer & equipment needed
- [ ] Set-up Email
- [ ] Set-up Vimeo
- [ ] Set-up Trello
- [ ] Software downloaded & ready to use
- [ ] Add to company calendar
- [ ] Send welcome email
    - [ ] Start date & time
    - [ ] What to bring
    - [ ] Parking
    - [ ] Attire

First day checklist

- [ ] Meet the team!
- [ ] Week's agenda
- [ ] Responsibilities
- [ ] Expectations
- [ ] How to use Trello, email server, Vimeo, etc.

☐ *Share codes and passwords*

☐ *Clocking in & out, if they are new to contract work*

☐ *Submitting timesheet / invoice procedure*

☐ *How to schedule time off*

☐ *Set meeting for 30-Day review*

☐ *List of employees and jobs*

First week checklist

☐ *Questions/concerns*

☐ *Review of first days*

First 30 days check-in *(30-day review)*

☐ *What's working*

☐ *What needs improvement*

☐ *Examine first projects*

☐ *Feedback from new employee*

☐ *Schedule 90-day review*

First 90 days check-in *(performance evaluation)*

☐ *Are tasks completed on time?*

☐ *Quality of work produced*

☐ *Attitude*

☐ *Positive feedback, areas to highlight*

☐ *Solicit feedback from other employees on performance*

☐ *Offer advice, encouragement and areas to improve*

☐ *Ask which tasks they've enjoyed and would enjoy working on moving forward*

☐ *Review things employees may need to be aware of over the next few weeks and months*

☐ *Set goals with the new employee to achieve maximum potential*

☐ *Plan moving forward*

⬇ Download a copy of this resource at UnifyYourMarketing.com

How to Schedule and Run Meetings With Your Team

Michael Hyatt and Co. published a book a few years ago called *No Fail Meetings*, and I highly recommend it. He was tired of wasted time, inefficiencies in his company, and lack of inspiration and direction once meetings were over. With his experience with running a large book publishing company for 14 years and then running his own business for nearly a decade, he has been in thousands of meetings.

He has five steps that frame how he shapes meetings that work:

1. *Decide.* What is going to be covered and who is going to attend

2. *Schedule.* With all involved parties at the right time and location

3. *Prepare.* What is the goal of the meeting and what items need to be covered? Use a results-driven agenda.

4. *Meet.* Always start the meeting with what the goal outcome of the meeting is. Be intentional, efficient, and productive

5. *Follow Up.* Review your notes on what tasks have been completed and what is still outstanding.

Michael also references using a template agenda so you can be guided by the template to move the meeting forward and stay on task. If you get derailed by another topic, give that topic a name, make note of it, and address it after the meeting. Give your team a sense of acknowledgment, but remind them that this isn't the objective of this current meeting.

I like scheduling touchpoint emails/texts/phone calls with my team members to check-in and remind them that I'm available to help serve them, and that I care about what they are working on.

My hope is that you can get the most out of your team meetings and continue to create buy-ins from your team and empower them to be solution finders within your organization.

CHAPTER 15

KEY TAKEAWAYS

Scale your team

- Knowing when it's time to hire
- Writing standard operating procedures
- The hiring process
- Onboarding checklist
- Scheduling and running meetings

SOUND THE TRUMPETS! (DOOT-DO-DO-DO!)

Release the doves! You have done it! Congratulations to you, your team, and your customers for having a better life! My god, what an accomplishment!

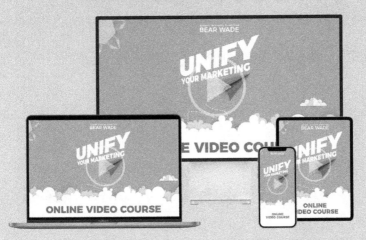

CONCLUSION

Revisit. Revise. Revamp.

Building a unified business isn't easy and if you remember at the beginning of this book I told you it was going to take tenacity. Well, you've done it.

I'm SO proud of you! This process is a crazy ride of emotions and grit, but look what you have built! This empire you have created is now unstoppable. You have built a legacy with this thing. This is something that can outlive you if you want it to. Don't forget to start working on a succession plan.

If you ever get stuck in your business, go back to the Brand Steps and try to diagnose your current situation, and work to mend your issues, and keep building something great! As you and your business grow, your perspective on different chapters will as well, so continue to use it as a guide in whatever comes your way.

For today, celebrate your success! Consider, now that you have a business that is "rawking", how are you going to change the world for the better with it?

You don't have to directly have a business that makes the impact, but I hope you help mentor others to build a company that can impact others for the better, and you use your wealth to impact the most people around you in a positive way.

Pass this book along to other entrepreneurs who could use a hand up and get the guidance that we all could have used when we started.

I can't wait to hear how your business has changed, and how your lifestyle has changed because of this.

We want to hear from you!

Send us your thoughts to: Success@UnifyYourMarketing.com

And remember, don't just check the boxes in your marketing. Unify it!

 VISIT US ONLINE

VISIT
UnifyYourMarketing.com

Download resources, explore the exercises reviewed in this book,
and view a list of references.

CPSIA information can be obtained
at www.ICGtesting.com
Printed in the USA
BVHW090905160921
616887BV00015B/377